Published on the occasion of the exhibition

Unexpected Pleasures:
The Art and Design of Contemporary Jewellery

National Gallery of Victoria, Melbourne
21 April – 26 August 2012

The Design Museum, London
5 December 2012 – 3 March 2013

This exhibition was organised by the Design Museum, London

UNEXPECTED PLEASURES

the art and design of

contemporary jewellery

Skira *Rizzoli* NEW YORK | DESIGN MUSEUM

TABLE OF CONTENTS

SECTION ONE
Texts

Foreword

Every so often the opportunity arises to have a conversation about contemporary jewellery and its place in the world. Unexpected Pleasures, The Art and Design of Contemporary Jewellery, is such a conversation, not only intended between jewellery makers and others in these fields, but also to engage with anyone who has a curiosity about contemporary jewellery. It presents a range of ideas and images about contemporary jewellery and design cast as an exhibition in the context of a design museum as a way of exploring the links between objects and everyday life. The intention behind this book is to explore how design and contemporary jewellery cross over with each other, and what each can offer the other to stretch their unique imagination. The conversation will be new for some readers, offer a different angle for others, and set up fresh discussion for those who think they may know all about contemporary jewellery.

The reader is first led through a series of discussions with different viewpoints about contemporary jewellery and its place in the world of art, design and craft. → 10 Deyan Sudjic talks about design as a way of seeing and understanding objects, with an emphasis on what we wear as creative expression. This lays the ground for my following discussion about the different experiences of contemporary jewellery. As a jeweller, I am acutely aware how contemporary jewellery will talk for both its maker and its wearer, and how these voices express different forms of belonging → 96 as a way to connect to those around us. Glenn Adamson challenges the intention of contemporary jewellers to contradict what jewellery should do and encourages a flourishing interchange between art, design and → 102 jewellery practices. Liesbeth den Besten discusses how contemporary jewellery has questioned—and skirted around—the concept of beauty, elaborating her observations in the context of the Dutch Galerie Ra. → 108 The final text, by the late Peter Dormer talks about the difficult relationship between contemporary jewellery and photography, and how the wearing of jewellery is often a very different experience to how jewellery is worn in a photograph.

The second part of this book celebrates the ideas expressed in contemporary jewellery and how they blur the boundaries of art, design, fashion and craft. This time the conversation focuses on how contemporary jewellery will speak for wearers about belonging in everyday contexts. It highlights how thinking and tactics about ideas are shared between makers. This provides a way to decode how jewellery is understood and at the same time puts into perspective our relationship with our everyday possessions. We are all wearers of objects in some way, and we freely sample from the world around us to reflect our basic human instinct for adornment. Contemporary jewellery stimulates a different experience of wearing objects, and, if nothing else, it will open up new conversations for its wearer.

The final part in the book completes an understanding of contemporary jewellery for those who know little about its origins. The conversation between contemporary jewellery, art and design is not a new one. But there are two things that mark this one as a key moment in time. Design is persuasive in our lives; so it is time now to engage a wider public in the conversation about contemporary jewellery and what it means to be contemporary. This is an endeavour that is being promoted by the Design Museum, which speaks of a need to re-evaluate what contemporary jewellery can offer us.

The conversation in this book is about aesthetics, possessions and belonging in our contemporary times, and it is shaped by the agendas of a contemporary jewellery maker and the Design Museum. Many experiences during this project, including this book, have been unexpected, and the pleasure for me has been how this opportunity has opened up different thinking. And I hope it leads to some unexpected pleasures for others.

CHAPTER ONE

The Art and Design of Contemporary Jewellery

Deyan Sudjic

Self-image is shaped, among other things, by a combination of gender, cultural identity, social conditioning and experience. These are aspects of the personality that are most clearly reflected by the things that we wear as well as by our possessions and, for want of a better word, by how we choose to adorn ourselves with them. Self-image is both an inescapable reflection of what and who we are and also a conscious choice that we make, and so in some senses is a quality that has been manufactured or, as you might say, that has been designed. But image can also be understood as being in itself a form of creative self-expression, one that goes beyond the simple act of consumption.

These are questions about the nature of identity that are anything but superficial. They occupy the fertile territory that spills over from fashion and into design, and then beyond that toward jewellery. And they are framed by other forms of visual culture, from art to architecture. Underlying them all is a search for a fundamental aspect of what it means to be human.

All of us have a need to mark and to remember the events that measure out our lives. We celebrate and we have regrets. We display our connectedness and our separateness from each other. We need to demonstrate our achievements, and sometimes our status and our wealth. And we choose to do all that in a manner which can be understood either directly or obliquely, which is in itself another kind of decision that sends out certain kinds of signals.

Objects are a form of communication that predates formal written languages. It is a kind of communication that, though expressed in different ways over time, remains essentially the same in its intentions. Some signals will be known only to initiates, others are more obvious, or at least more universally understood. The paradoxical category in this is that of discretion. Is this to be understood as polite restraint, or is it a kind of private language?

Finding ways to explore and to understand the many meanings of objects has formed a significant strand of design criticism since at least the time of Adolf Loos. Despite the fundamentalist puritanism that the cartoon-strip version of his most celebrated essay, "Ornament and Crime", with its strictures against tattoos, is purported to represent, Loos had a subtle and nuanced appreciation of the nature of material culture and modernity. His writings had a remarkable clarity and wit, and they have set an agenda for our understanding of the place of design in the contemporary landscape.

Loos approached the modern world with the inquiring mind and the clear sight of a social anthropologist. He was fascinated by everything around him in Vienna, a city that in 1900 was going through change at an unprecedented speed. He was interested in such diverse issues as the length that men and women should wear their hair and how the norms that govern their decision have changed over time. He wrote about the number of pleats in a Norfolk jacket and the significance of the patterns on his shoe leather. He was continually scornful of what he represented as being a form of Austrian backwardness and an enthusiast for what he took to be English aristocratic restraint.

Writing at about the same time as Loos, the maverick American economist Thorstein Veblen invented the term *conspicuous consumption* to describe the way that objects from furniture to jewellery are put to work for social and economic purposes. Veblen put forward his view of what he called the theory of the leisure class, suggesting that most societies develop hierarchies which privilege those castes and occupations that do not require manual labour above those that do. At the apex of such systems are the warriors and priests, and some form of aristocracy; at the base are the workers, and in the middle can be found the merchants. Given such a hierarchy, those art forms that have no obvious sign of utility have a tendency to be presented in such a way as to suggest a higher level of prestige than those that carry the burden of being useful. Art is categorised as fine art, as opposed to an applied, decorative or commercial art, terms that can be seen as differentiating it from the real thing. Fine art enjoys a status different from that of design.

Veblen used these concepts to interpret the ways in which we use possessions, both practically and symbolically. He was also fascinated by the visual signals that we use to judge quality, and which shape our aesthetic responses. In Veblen's view, objects that reflect well on their owners need to demonstrate quality, and the visible investment of the resources of time and labour. In this sense the handmade, because it involves the conspicuous use of labour, has higher status than the machine-made, even though it performs its functional purpose less well. As Veblen puts it,

"the cheap, and therefore indecorous, articles of daily consumption in modern industrial communities are commonly machine products; and the generic feature of the physiognomy of machine-made goods as compared with the hand-wrought article is their greater perfection in workmanship and greater accuracy in the detail execution of the design. Hence it comes about that the visible imperfections of the hand-wrought goods, being honorific, are accounted marks of superiority in point of beauty, or serviceability, or both. Hence has arisen that exaltation of the defective, of which John Ruskin and William Morris were such eager spokesmen in their time; and on this ground their propaganda of crudity and wasted effort has been taken up and carried forward since their time. And hence also the propaganda for a return to handicraft and household industry. So much of the work and speculations of this group of men as fairly comes under the characterization here given would have been impossible at a time when the visibly more perfect goods were not the cheaper."

Sixty years after Adolf Loos's essays first appeared, the British architectural critic Reyner Banham took a similarly acute, just as creative and equally acid interest in the tribal rituals of contemporary culture. In his case, he was looking at the way that drivers on Californian freeways adjusted their appearances before reaching surface streets, at how the culture of surf-board customisers developed, and the social significance of carrying a clipboard—or, as Banham called it, "the power plank".

I was born in England in the 1950s and went to an all-male selective school in London. It is not entirely surprising, then, that I have a fairly specific set of preconceptions about adornment. I tell myself from time to time that I am not the kind of person to wear jewellery. It is not the way that I see myself. People like me don't do that kind of thing, and I am, of course, quite wrong: actually, all of us do just that. It's just that jewellery might take on different forms.

As an adolescent growing up at the end of the 1960s, I remember that, along with the cloud of patchouli, there was a certain amount of enthusiasm for making stove-enamelled rings, for single-shark-tooth necklaces and beaded wristbands, for puzzle rings, for the single earring; all of them the signs of dissent and a taste for the exotic. They went nicely with sheepskin coats from Afghanistan, mirrored Moroccan-leather shoulder bags, and carrying a copy of Bob Dylan's *Blonde on Blonde* double album under the arm. A gold chain around the neck, a signet ring on the appropriate finger, a belt buckle, a tie pin, or for that matter a tie, can all be more than enough to place their wearers in a precise social context—just as a fraternity ring is as essential for middle-class Americans, as a stars-and-stripes pin is an indispensable prop for American presidential candidates. Being a conventional kind of an Englishman, I do not wear a wedding ring. Less conventionally, I do not have a watch. And, save for the most exceptional occasions, I have no cuff-links to tether the extremities of my shirts. But of course I do, whether I like it or not, whether I intend to or not, in fact, wear jewellery.

The key question is: what do we mean by *jewellery*? There are so many definitions that go beyond the archetype of the ring, the necklace and the bracelet. I have to depend on my spectacles to read the small print when I go to see any of the myriad of consultants that form the daily background to life as a museum director. And even before I can get to meet them, I find myself being asked in the name of security precautions, to come to terms with an object that can also be understood as an item of jewellery, something that requires me to consider certain words from a new and somewhat unfamiliar perspective.

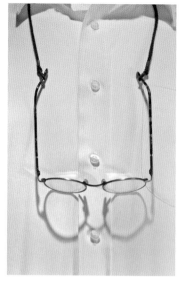

Habitually wearing spectacles around the neck makes them a variety of necklace.

The lanyard can be worn on the lapel
or around the neck or waist.

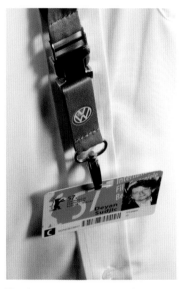

The clips, straps and buckles reinforce the
message of authority.

Lanyard is a curious, hard to grasp kind of word, one that belongs to a category of objects that is unfamiliar to those without a specialist interest in the field to which it belongs—in this case, sailing. The nautical origins of the lanyard suggest precision and skill. But the term has come to mean something rather different to what it was once understood to signify, and it is the one that most clearly demonstrates how the security tag is becoming a de facto piece of jewellery. *Lanyard* has come to mean the rope that tethers or connects an object to the person. And it is that link to the body that is the essential qualification an object needs to be understood as a piece of jewellery.

Lanyard used to be the word to describe the salt-encrusted ropes seamen deployed to thread through a pair of deadeyes to adjust the rigging of a sailing vessel. The lanyard managed to survive long past the age of sail. It later went on to be applied to almost any kind of cord. It was a string that could be passed around the neck, shoulder or wrist to be used for the purpose of keeping a knife or whistle in place or, in the case of the British military police in the middle of the twentieth-century, a Webley service revolver. Such knives, whistles and revolvers quickly atrophied from actual weapons to ceremonial accoutrements. This kind of lanyard metamorphosed from a useful piece of practical equipment to become a part of the conventional repertoire of uniform making, as much an empty symbol as epaulets, medal ribbons, gold braid and brass buttons.

These are associations for the lanyard that suggest, respectively, competence, skill and expertise under fire on the one hand, and signals of authority and rank on the other.

A new but clearly related meaning for the word has emerged. It draws on all those associations, even if it does so in a way that might be understood as diminishing them in its embrace. The British Labour Party—or as Tony Blair, the Prime Minister of the day, insisted on styling it, New Labour—attracted sceptical attention for putting one of its less-than-appropriate corporate sponsors' logos on what it had called the lanyards on the security passes that all delegates had to wear to secure admission to one or other of its party conferences. It was all so much more impressive sounding than selling advertising space on a piece of string, even if, in the juxtaposition of the essentially sedentary nature of a party delegate's duties and the physical skills required to manipulate the rigging of a ship under sail, it did run the risk of sounding just a little ridiculous.

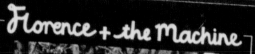

The elevation of the string that keeps a security pass in position in the staff canteen to the status of a massive rope snaking across a heaving deck was the crystallisation of a phenomenon that had been quietly building for some time. It marked the transformation of something as essentially utilitarian as a pass into an object that, whether consciously intended or not, will be worn on the body to signify status and record an event and adorn the body. Equally, the categories of object that we regard as more conventional forms of jewellery can also be understood as once having gone through a similar transformation to the one made by the pass and the lanyard.

There are functional or semi-functional origins for most forms of adornment that in time go through a metamorphosis from the practical to the symbolic. The domestication of the lanyard and its celebration through the brash heraldry of sponsors' logos, as if it were a football shirt, invites us to think again about exactly what it means to wear these plastic cards, often embellished by a photograph and sometimes by a holographic seal, around the neck or clipped to the waist or to the jacket lapel. Sometimes they are held in place by little metallic chains, sometimes on the sturdy flat rope or the lanyard, which itself was decorated by the sponsor's logo and designed to be read from a long way off by television cameras.

These are clearly artefacts that are to be understood on a number of different levels that go somewhat beyond simple utility. In any case, they are to be understood as something rather more dignified than the mute polythene envelope that contains the torn-off, hurriedly filled-out form that has been completed by a temporary visitor. The security tag can be regarded as a badge of servitude—the mark of an employee tethered to their employer, the daily price of admission to the work-place, both in a literal and a symbolic sense. Almost always, they are ugly and crudely fashioned.

And yet they are also a reflection of privileged participation in a special event. The party conference delegates can consider themselves as belonging to an elite… and how much more so can the holder of a plastic rectangle marked by the words *access all areas* at a music festival. The badge is the mark of belonging.

Closely related to it is the ski-lift pass, for which special jacket pockets and retractable mechanisms for the lanyard offer handy props. The passes that flight crew are required to wear in order to pass through security checkpoints at airports are another close cousin of the type. It is interesting to note, however, that such passes are not generally deployed by soldiers on the field of battle, even if they have name tags sewn into their uniforms and identity bracelets—also known as dog tags, dangling from neck chains.

Military dog tags have a bleak mission when necessary to identify casualties. "Access all areas" is more benign.

The badge could be understood as the latest descendant of the medal, which is also not worn in combat. Any medal is to be understood as a piece of jewellery, in that it is intended as a means of marking significant events, both public and private. The medal as a type has a long and distinguished history, which has involved many very talented artists in the past. Perhaps in the same way that portraiture has for the most part declined into mush, if we are to judge by the published designs for the London Olympic medals have deteriorated into creative senility. It was not always that way.

The Iron Cross, the German military medal for valour, for example, has its roots in the Prussian kingdom's life-and-death struggle with Napoleon. William III commissioned the distinguished architect Karl Friedrich Schinkel, responsible for some of Berlin's greatest landmarks, to devise an appropriate decoration. Schinkel's medal drew on the imagery of chivalric heraldry that looked back as far as Teutonic participation in the Crusades. It referred to an aggressive warrior class that set out to conquer huge swathes of territory in East Prussia, but it was only in Hitler's time that the medal was contaminated by the addition of the swastika.

The Iron Cross was also, in a sense, democratic, in that it was a decoration intended to transcend social status as it was open to all ranks. And it was also intended, through embellishment, from adornment with stylised oak leaves, diamonds and gold, to be adapted and personalised to reflect a range of achievements and specific events.

Schinkel's medal was also innovative in its use of humble materials. A cross made of iron underscored that it was the qualities of its recipients that conferred prestige on the medal, rather than the other way around. Joining the ranks of the heroes is what made the Iron Cross so valued, not the inherent qualities of the materials of which it is made. From a technical point of view, the cross depended on finding a satisfactory way to combine iron with the silver edge that Schinkel designed for it. No easy task, given that soldering the two materials together was a near physical impossibility. Instead, the Prussians had to find a way of making the silver edge into a kind of frame.

Not all medals are created equal. Some, the Victoria Cross for example, retain a sense of relating only to the highest achievements. They are rare and exceptional. Others are issued to mark a campaign, a victory or simply long service, and their holders may run into the hundreds of thousands. But jewellery is also used to mark precisely the course of such events.

Medals have a history as ancient as jewellery, of which they must be considered a subset.

Fascinatingly as the hierarchy of medals has developed, so there are now some carefully delineated signifiers for the signifiers. The medal ribbon—or should that be lanyard—has taken on a life of its own independent of the medal it was designed to carry. Military uniforms are now marked by rectangular strips of colour, which sometimes seem to run to several paragraphs across the chest as symbolic representations of the absent medals themselves, building up over the course of a military career, like collections of air miles. Russian veterans of the Red Army conventionally opt for wearing the medals themselves, even while in civilian clothes, while in Britain when the Queen bestows a minor decoration, the medal ribbon has already been shrunk from a textile long enough to place around the neck to a miniature version, just sufficient in length to dangle from a safety pin attached to the lapel of a jacket. American detectives have gone in the opposite direction. For them, the badge of office has migrated from the chest, pinned Western-sheriff style, into a leather holster slung around the neck.

Until now, there has been at least one significant difference between the medal and the security pass. The medal was always a self-conscious piece of design, or even an aspect of a minor art form. The security tag at its humblest is an anonymous piece of manufacturing. It depends on off-the-shelf components, assembled in their millions that cost almost nothing, and which can be treated as disposable.

There are now a wider range of approaches, relying on more self-conscious design work. Graphic designers have started to treat the see-through plastic rectangle as a distinct medium, much as the album cover once was. The act of party-conference going includes a number of physical rituals, of which the procession from conference hotel to conference hall under the gaze of television cameras is just the most conspicuous. The lanyard and the badge are the price of admission. The badge can also be a sign of authority: think about the way that senior British immigration officials standing behind their more junior colleagues seated at the counters at Heathrow wear them to distinguish themselves from the civilians.

The nature of that word *lanyard* gives a hint of what is going on. It is presenting the security badge as if it were a vital piece of equipment, on a level with the policeman's whistle, and the service revolver. But these items too can be understood as much as ceremonial badges of office, no less than the security tag. The way that they are worn, displayed and embellished has as much to do with status, self image and rank as with anything more utilitarian.

What has happened in the last fifty years is that the contemporary incarnation of jewellery has used these conventions to question their basis, to interrogate and to undermine the signs of authority and value. And yet these signifiers still reflect positively on those with the courage and the insight to wear them. They imply a special form of knowledge that marks the wearer as one who understands the message carried by the object, and so who is set apart from those without such an insight. And also like jewellery, these signifiers are the marks that show who belongs and who does not belong.

Equally, these are the attributes and the messages that can be carried by a range of objects that can be understood not as jewellery but as design. But jewellery, because it is less rooted in an industrial system than, say, a wristwatch or a pair of headphones, is more able to take on transgressive meanings, to act, in fact, as works of critical design, which ask questions without necessarily answering them—a habit that design is sometimes too eager to do.

The gradual introduction of the pass reflects the transformation of twenty-first century attitudes to security and identity. And as the pass has become more and more universal, so it has come to take on roles other than those for which it was originally intended. It now tends to be worn not just in the workplace. If that workplace has the potential to offer the wearer a certain reflected glory, then the badge is displayed elsewhere. For a designer to take into account all these phenomena, some material, some social, and then to use the rope as a means for portable advertising is based on a sophisticated conception of how such images are understood. And it allows an insight into the nature of the relationship between object and individual.

Before I heard the word *lanyard* used in connection with any kind of a security pass, I had seen Susan Cohn's work. She is a jeweller who has also worked as a designer. Traditionally, there have been sharp divisions between these two categories. Not least because industrial design in its modernist phase did all that it could to present itself as concerned with objective reality rather than with emotions. It sought to distance itself from the subjectivity of jewellery and all forms of what are labelled crafts. It did all that it could to remove the mark of the maker's hand, in pursuit of the assumption of perfection that is regarded as the product of the machine-made object, rather contrary to Thorstein Veblen's beliefs.

One of a series of watches designed for LIP by Roger Tallon. Note the three prominent balls.

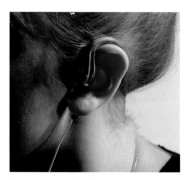

Above and right: Headphones are now carefully designed as items of adornment.

In fact, this was as much an emotional objective as one based on practicalities. The smooth forms and the precision conventionally associated with machines are usually the product of labour-intensive finishing techniques. The modern movement attempted to present design as a process of problem solving. Pose the right question, it was suggested, and design can offer the appropriate solution. And there is a long history of poets and philosophers who have suggested that truth and beauty are intimately connected.

But there are so many objects that we humans want to possess that are not the answer to any kind of problem. They are simply things that we want to have rather than that we need. Or perhaps human needs extend beyond the most obvious practical forms of survival. We have emotional needs as well as physical ones, and design has shifted its ground to embrace this ancient role.

The supposed boundary between function and emotion was never as clear-cut as the rhetoric of functionalism would have had us believe. Modernism always had its poetic aspects. Purity and ideal form are not necessarily the product of a pragmatic approach to mechanisation, but, have left a mark on the way that we regard other forms of object making.

Industrial design has certainly had an enormous impact on our visual imagination—how could it not have? A manufacturing process resulted in such remarkable objects as a Boeing 747, a lunar lander, an Eames lounger, and Robin Day's design for polypropylene stacking chair, objects that are so sculpturally powerful and so charismatic that they cannot but have had an important impact on the parameters within which design, sculpture and craft, and jewellery operate—and so in the way that so many objects look.

These are also objects for which skill and precision are qualities that matter, even if they are not conventionally considered part of the repertoire of adornment. These materials need to find ways in which they can take on the qualities of jewellery, to find a form of expression that brings out their material qualities in ways that make something of their potential. Acrylic plastics needed designers to find ways to work them and mould them to give them positive rather than negative connotations that were once associated with plastics.

Industrial manufacturing provides the visual clues, the techniques and the parameters to which makers and jewellers cannot but respond any less than art cannot but respond to the visual language of its time. These objects made with sophisticated production techniques have so much power and charisma that they cannot but provide visual clues of one kind of another that shape the individual maker's visual imagination for better or worse. These are shapes and techniques that redefine the centre of gravity of a creative approach.

Sony's Walkman defined personal electronics as more than an appliance.

The lapel mic: a badge of office and a sign of connectedness.

Where we keep our sunglasses is a personal decision.

Cohn is certainly a jeweller rather than a designer, but she was also one of the many individuals that Alberto Alessi sought out to commission to work for his company to produce an object that can only be described as design, even if it is based on ideas she had previously explored in her jewellery work, albeit in perforated stove-coloured steel. And beyond that, I had seen the pieces she made based on her close observation of the way that we all consciously or unconsciously make use of every-day artefacts intended to be worn on the body: spectacles, sunglasses, lapel microphones and so many others. These are objects whose roots are in a different world from what was once understood to be the one defined by jewellery. They are made for different purposes. They are co-opted by their wearers. Often they are produced by designers, who find their work being transformed into something that is rather different from what they had originally intended. Equally, they may be knowingly crafted to exploit the potential of their unofficial role. Either way, they have invaded the territory that jewellery had always seen as its own preserve.

Cohn's observational pieces made me think about jewellery in a way that I had not considered before. And they also made me think about design in a way that was new for me. It gave me the sense that both sides of this division between what are conventionally called design and jewellery are more connected than they sometimes seem. The essence of the skills that underpin jewellery has much to teach designers. These are the issues that can inform a design that depends for its meaning on the way that an object is touched or worn or experienced. But there is also much that those who craft jewellery have to learn from industrially manufactured objects, as well as from the rituals that grow up around them and their use.

What really sets jewellery apart from many forms of design is its acceptance of the body as its starting point. Industrial designers have a lot to learn about the impact of the human body on their work from the way that jewellers understand them. When Jonathan Ive and his team at Apple set about the design work that would eventually see them manufacturing black polycarbonate MacBook laptop-computer shells, they did not foresee the speed with which the finger marks left by skin oils would undermine the initial perfection of the object. Oil from skin leaves marks that burn into the smooth surface of most plastics, unless they have been appropriately treated. The sheen of the industrial object is almost instantly compromised when it is subjected to the grasp of those that it is intended to lure.

If this were a deliberate strategy devised by a designer attempting to bite the hand of the corporation that was feeding him, it could be judged as an effective piece of critical design, a commentary on the nature of consumption. It would be a knowing understanding of the nature of material qualities and putting them to work for a purpose, as Susan Cohn did when she anodised aluminium rings black, well aware they would not stay pristine for long but would start to deform and mark with use, the scratches and dents gradually revealing the metal beneath the surface, and so creating an object that is able to mark the passing of time. But the scarring of the MacBook's surface was an unintended consequence, rather than the predicted outcome of a deliberate decision.

Ive's team learned the practical lessons of polycarbonate shells for their later products quickly. The MacBook Pro, which comes with what Apple calls a unibody structure, is a remarkable example of production technology pushed into new directions. Making the body of the machine begins from raw aluminium, which is extruded and then milled. The surface doesn't show finger marks. The key-board shrugs off the dandruff that collects on polycarbonate machines, because there is no static charge. The material qualities of the self-finished aluminium body maintain their characteristics for much longer than its predecessor.

They still don't have the emotional content of Cohn's black ring, though, where use leaves the marks of character. In itself, it is a piece of jewellery that owes something to her observation of some of the more appealing aspects of material behaviour. The black paint used to finish the brass body of a 35 mm single-lens reflex camera from the 1960s was not intended to chip. But as it did, it gradually revealed traces of a bright metal gleaming beneath. On one level it was deteriorating. But on another it was maturing and, in so doing, acquiring a kind of patina. And it was one that Cohn worked on to give her rings. As yet, there are few examples of industrial designers self-consciously attempting to do the same. The most likely approach is the pragmatism of Kenneth Grange, who, when he was designing cigarette lighters with polycarbonate bodies, got around the finger-marking problem by tumbling the mouldings in a drum of walnut shells, leaving an invisible film that protected them from marking.

The cultural history of the relationship between jewellery, art and design is not straightforward. They are able to learn from one another. And there are certain areas which can be described as cross-over territory, the wrist-watch for example. Others, such as spectacles, in which the original forms were devised by designers, are now explored as archetypes to be subverted by jewellers looking to take the impact of their modification of the body to its logical conclusion.

The Braun cigarette lighter became a signifier.

Opposite: Nikons in the days of film lasted long enough to grow old gracefully.

There are some designers able to operate in the field of jewellery, and some jewellers who can make industrial design. But at some times during the modern period it has seemed as if jewellery was a medium that was being used by designers to convey a message about what was essentially something else. Just as architects from Charles Rennie Mackintosh to Le Corbusier to Robert Venturi have been fascinated by the potential of chairs to encapsulate the essence of their architectural ideas, so jewellery has been put to work in a similar way.

The Viennese architect Josef Hoffmann's working programme for the Wiener Werkstätte drawn up in 1905 discussed jewellery:

"We use many semiprecious stones. They make up in beauty of colour and infinite variety what they lack in value by comparison with diamonds. The worth of artistic work and of inspiration must be recognised and prized once again".

But what the Werkstätte produced in the way of jewellery was no more than a restatement of the aesthetic values that were developed to shape its architectural spaces. Adolf Loos, no friend of the Werkstätte, took a more austere view of decoration and ornament. But look at the Post Office Savings Bank, Otto Wagner's masterpiece, and it is not hard to see it as a piece of architecture that has been treated with the finesse of a jeweller. How else can you interpret the way in which its white marble surface is embellished with aluminium studs? They suggest adornment, but they also reveal a lot about the essential nature of the way in which the architect has understood the art of construction.

There have, however, been moments when jewellery has been energised and invigorated by creative input from other directions. When Alexander Calder worked on making a necklace, he was more emotionally engaged with the material than the Hoffmann workshop had been. And he was ready to incorporate found fragments as well as precious metal. So was Charlotte Perriand. Not only did she use ball bearings in one case and sea shells in another to make necklaces, there is also a remarkable prefiguration of contemporary jewellery's interest in photography in her work. Perriand's most enduring piece of furniture is the chaise longue, with its chrome-plated steel runners that she designed with Le Corbusier and Pierre Jeanneret. And the most well-known image of it has Perriand herself leaning back on its undulating form. Her head is turned provocatively away from the camera, face hidden, but the ball bearings around her neck are clearly visible. For Perriand, the edges between art and design and the conceptual thinking that underpins jewellery were far from rigid.

There are other designers who have shared this range. Throughout his long career, the Italian architect and designer Ettore Sottsass was able to bring an emotional intensity to all the objects that he worked on, from furniture to glass and to jewellery. Sottsass moved from designing main-frame computers and typewriters to glass, ceramics, and jewellery with remarkable fluency. For Sottsass, a ring was rather more than a miniature platform to demonstrate an aesthetic that he had already developed for a chair; it was a way to channel his ideas about people and their relationship with things into a number of highly charged objects. In the end, Sottsass was a blend of artist and designer with the courage to tackle almost anything and to resolve it with conviction. Sottsass was also fascinated by the heritage of Indian culture and mysticism that informed much of his work and gave it a ritual aspect.

I remember being struck forcibly by the redefinition and deconstruction of jewellery back in the 1970s by an exhibition of the work of Gijs Bakker. What Bakker had done was called jewellery, but all that there was to see was a collection of photographs of people holding cigarette packets. You didn't have to fold it into the sleeve of your tee shirt James Dean style to use a Marlboro pack as an item of adornment. He caught the way that we hold packs in one hand or both hands. He tracked the way that we put them down on tables. He looked at the colour, the shape and the way that we open the box, the way that we rotate it. He regarded these activities as, in themselves, an act of design.

Bakker has been an unusual figure in his ability to transcend cultural boundaries. He was trained both as a jeweller and as an industrial designer. He was designing chairs for mass production back in the 1970s. But he was also exploring a new definition of the meaning of jewellery, and in the process he joined a group that was giving the form a vitality and energy that other forms of work that involved handcraft came to lack. In those days, with the exhibitions that he made that toured Europe, he was making more of a contribution to what we can understand as jewellery. Later he was the cofounder of Droog design, which was to have a huge impact in redefining the role of what can be expected of design, not only through his own work, but also by bringing together a cluster of designers who were ready to discuss a form of design that could be both pragmatic and playful.

The relationship, conscious and unconscious, between designed objects, which are presented as a category of things entirely distinct from jewellery and what is described as jewellery is a fascinating one. Flesh-coloured radio mikes and Apple's wearable iPods that are more or less knowingly designed as if they were jewellery, are one example. That is to say, they have a scale and an attention to detail that reflects their close connection with the human body. They are designed to be worn; they are designed as a kind of adornment.

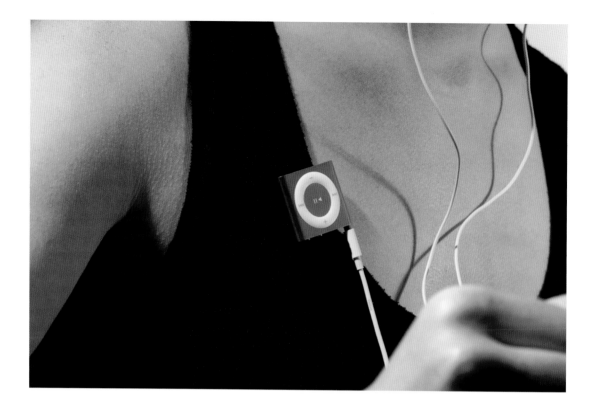

Contemporary jewellery has the ability and the intellectual energy to provide a critical commentary to certain aspects of design. In particular, a piece of contemporary jewellery has the charisma and the presence to allow for the deconstruction of the way design has taken on a role as a status signifier. The jeweller can pull us all up short through the way that observes our social rituals. And not just observes: jewellery still has the authenticity to shape as well as to reflect in the objects that they make and point out to us. Jewellery gives us grounding in time. It reminds us how our relationship with our possessions follows long-established patterns. Jewellers have been shaping these possessions for very much longer than designers have. They have responded to the search for ways in which objects can carry meaning and reflect gender and value. And jewellery maintains an individual relationship between maker and wearer that mass production associated with industrial design can't.

Like dance or art, jewellery has been with mankind since its earliest days. Design belongs to a more recent evolution, to the idea of an industrial culture. This is a phase in human development that in fact may have deeper roots than is sometimes acknowledged. The amphora and the coin have certainly been mass-produced… and so designed, for a couple of millennia before what we think of as the Industrial Revolution. Through jewellery, the atavistic tendencies that have shaped our worlds and our lives keep resurfacing. The balance between those who describe themselves as jewellers and those who work as designers is shifting. In the preindustrial age, design meant something very different from what it does when the connection between maker and patron has been severed by mass production and machinery.

When Apple migrated the iPod to the lapel, they crossed the role of industrial designer with jeweller.

The form of the microphone keeps shifting into territory occupied both by jewellery and prosthetics.

Before the machine age, the jeweller had the role of making certain objects that play the same role that designed objects have in the present day. In our era, jewellers have become less central figures in the industrial system, and yet they have much to offer to those who chose to define themselves as designers rather than as makers. The issue is how much design can ask questions about the system that brings it into being. It is a part of that system in the way that jewellery need not be. The objects that a jeweller makes exist in a context in which it is economically feasible to make objects that are challenging and questioning.

Jewellery in the way that Cohn works with it is not in fact mass-produced; it is made by hand and depends on specific skills. It can aspire to the tactile qualities of industrial design but still find the room to question its most fundamental assumptions. It is an economic model that was taken up by a generation trained as industrial designers either unwilling to work within the industrial-manufacturing context or else unable to find the way to do so, who began to explore the idea of what might better be called batch production than the limited edition.

To make in small numbers objects that either do not require costly tooling or which, through a process of creative scavenging, can offer tactile qualities of equivalent sophistication in the context of a workshop was a survival strategy adopted by designers from Ron Arad to Jasper Morrison. They were not interested in the ideology conjured up by the fetishisation of the concept of making, but they could create the aura of an authoritative industrial object through their skills and conceptual imagination in a way that jewellery had continued to do.

And jewellery at the same time managed to maintain a grip on relevance in which many craft skills-based makers have not. The bookbinder, the calligrapher and the potter have struggled to maintain the grip on the imagination that certain forms of jewellery have continued to do.

Jewellery has proved itself to have an unexpected staying power against a background in which so many of what are conventionally described as the crafts have atrophied. What it has in its favour is the way that it speaks so directly to the rituals of human life. Design has a lot to learn from this, even as it becomes ever closer to the roots of economic and industrial power.

Susan Cohn

Susan Cohn works both as a jeweller and a designer. In addition to the jewellery commissions carried out in her Melbourne, Australia, workshop, she has also worked for Alessi, which makes her designs. The works are not always mass-produced, but they are made in small groups using industrial methods.

Cohn is fascinated by the interplay between design and jewellery. She explores the relationship between people and their possessions, looking for the ways in which individuals use their material objects to send signals about how they see their place in the world. Sometimes she makes observational pieces: *Access All Areas* monumentalises the security pass and demonstrates how a banal, everyday object can take on a different level of meaning. Its relationship to the body is what gives it the quality of jewellery because, unlike a credit card, it is intended to be worn. Cohn is interested in understanding the issues that are important to designers: how value is conveyed and the way in which objects age. Her black rings, for example, are deliberately intended to mark the passage of time as their painted surface degrades.

OPPOSITE · Susan Cohn · *Scim Rings* · 2003–ongoing ·
Rings · Anodised aluminium, enamel paint · 10 × 4 mm × various diameters

TOP LEFT · Susan Cohn · *Security Pass* · 1989 ·
Security pass · Anodised aluminium · 155 × 56 × 24 mm

TOP RIGHT · Susan Cohn · *Cohncave* · in production since 1992
Bowl · Powder-coated steel · 480 × 480 × 75 mm diameter ·
Made by Alessi, Crusinallo, Italy

BOTTOM RIGHT · Susan Cohn · *Torn Mesh Bracelet* · 1989 ·
Bracelet · Anodised aluminium, 750 gold · 320 × 320 × 35 mm

CHAPTER TWO

Making, Wearing, Belonging

Susan Cohn

I have always been fascinated with how jewellery speaks to and for people. Jewellery is a dynamic force in everyday life, with a rich emotional vocabulary employed by people to connect intimately and publicly. Jewellery can draw attention to our sexuality, enhance our beauty, show off wealth, signal status or project power. These gestures depend on the maker, who works to embody ideas through form and materials, and the wearer, who charges jewellery with life.

When worn, jewellery speaks for us with intimate inflection: "I want, therefore I am". It revels in uncovering our personal stories, betrays us by speaking of our deepest wants and collaborates in sly diversions from our most delicate truths. Other possessions may be abandoned after use without a second thought, but jewellery retains an emotional value long after its novelty has worn off. With its own secret life, it can evoke the past, highlight the present and even provoke future fantasies.

My interests as a maker are inseparable from my social instincts. Through years of practice I have developed a kind of voyeurism based around jewellery's codes. I am always attuned to the ways jewellery is "lived", co-opted as part of our daily routines, conversations, displays and transgressions. A focus on craftsmanship, precious materials and the beauty in making will only uncover the more visible dimension in jewellery's relationship to people.

While many of the personal possessions we pursue will be abandoned after use without a second thought, jewellery retains an emotional value long after its novelty has worn off. Perhaps this is because it becomes so deeply embedded in the daily games of life. Often without conscious intent, jewellery is used to draw attention to sexuality or to enhance beauty, show off wealth, signal status and project power. To some extent, these gestures depend on the maker, who works to embody ideas through form and materials. But, ultimately, it is the wearer who gives jewellery its secret life. Whether reveling in unconscious revelations or collaborating in sly diversions from the truth, jewellery speaks for people with intimate inflection: "I want, therefore I am."

Perhaps the most engaging aspect of jewellery lies not in its more apparent values but in the inconsistent details that can be so easy to miss. These are the moments when a simple ring, or twist of a ring, can signal an intention, reinforce an attachment, suggest a secret to be betrayed, or make a comment without saying very much at all. Such flashes are often marked on the object worn, in nicks and scuffs that might be considered to detract from the precious quality of other designed objects. But jewellery is precious *because* it traces the contours of our past. Time is commissioned as an active agent in its meaning-making. Even the marks can become precious, impregnated with some memory or association, held dear as a personal sign of difference.

It is clear that jewellery is distinct, but what is its relationship to the other kinds of objects that we wear and carry? Roland Barthes saw jewellery not simply as an item of style, but the "detail", the "next-to-nothing", the "detached term" that links style's elements together with meaning.[1] Barthes turned his gaze to jewellery as a way to comprehend greater change. At the time of writing—1961—new openings in appearance, fashion and domestic life were laying bare a shift in developed cultures and societies. To Barthes' mind, jewellery's role in style perfectly suggested a growing desire by society to define individual taste amid a barrage of mass-media images, consumer products and lifestyles.

Barthes recognised that the "poetic imagination" of jewellery in modern times was undergoing a profound transformation. Jewellery, he observed, had traditionally meant gemstones, with all they implied—the inhuman power and infernal quality of gems, so precious and pure but loaded with femme-fatale powers of seduction. Barthes knew that jewellery's status in modern times was beginning to unravel in a world pushing for change. There has been "a widespread liberation of jewellery" he wrote. It is now "an object that is free, if one can say this, from prejudice: multiform, multisubstance, to be used in an infinite variety of ways, it is now no longer subservient to the law of the highest price nor that of being used in only one way, such as for a party of sacred occasion: jewellery has become democratic."[2]

Contemporary jewellery started as a movement among makers seeking to recode what jewellery is and how it can express value

Barthes wrote in the same year as the first major show of contemporary jewellery took place, at Goldsmith's Hall in London, more than ten years before the emergence of the Contemporary Jewellery Movement.

Contemporary jewellery started as a movement among makers seeking to recode what jewellery is and how it can express value. In a decade when cultural resistance and artistic experimentation reshaped popular culture, jewellers sought to relieve jewellery of its deep economic imprint. They rebelled against jewellery's expected pleasures, its narrow conception as a luxury item given ceremoniously on special occasions.

The Contemporary Jewellery Movement provided the foundations for a creative field that maintains great vitality today. From the start of the movement, makers had built on early experimentation and thinking as the basis for concerted social and artistic action. They questioned the relevance of precious materials in jewellery and showed that any idea, material, form or technology could be used in creating jewellery that acquires preciousness from personal association rather than intrinsic value. What mattered to these makers was that jewellery be accessible to everyone, regardless of age, gender or class. They explored jewellery as an experience and a performance making visible its vital relationship to the body.

Unexpected Pleasures is an exploration of contemporary jewellery. The term is complicated and difficult. In this essay it is used to refer separately and at once to a family of objects, a making tradition, an historical movement, an established profession and a field of people currently engaged as either makers or spectators.

Contemporary jewellery could be understood as a game in which to play. Like a ball or a playing card, works are used to express skill and status, to define competition and to show off successful strategies.

→ 116
→ 156
The *Worn Out* and *Linking Links* sections of this book show that tactics on the playing field may belong to individual makers, but they also drive resemblances between works and approaches. In *Linking Links* especially I have sought to draw links between works based on common creative strategies or social thinking.

The exhibition on which this book is based is cast through my own perspective as a maker and informed by a tacit knowledge of how different approaches to making speak for people. I must admit that my engagement with other makers' work is usually mediated by my own interests, and my first instinct is always to question how the wearer is considered as part of the creative process. I relish observing the endless ways a wearer can charge jewellery with meaning. Without their intervention the object appears inert, an object-in-waiting. I recognise that this is not the view of all makers—in fact, the wearer is frequently not the focus in contemporary jewellery works, shows and surveys.

The thinking behind *Unexpected Pleasures* has benefited from many conversations that I could never have anticipated before embarking on this exploration. Just like making jewellery, in making this exhibition, I have had to work within certain design parameters to realize my ideas. How to place contemporary jewellery within a design museum, where there is less attention placed on the values of the original object? My solution is to highlight the relationships invested within the works—that is, how they might speak of belonging for the jewellers, who talk to each other through the making, and for wearers, who bring into the equation an entirely different set of relationships and expectations.

The exhibition has a broad conceptual base drawing on work from around the world and from different times. In this book, as in the exhibition that shares its name, I am concerned to refer back to the past only so far as it may help us to understand the present. The experience is cast from two polar perspectives. *Worn Out* highlights the experience of wearing as central to appreciating experimentation in contemporary jewellery. *Linking Links* focuses on the finished object as a window onto the experience of making. Each jewellery object embodies the interests of a maker, not only in respect to craftsmanship and design values but also as a response to jewellery's many social roles.

In the *Linking Links* section, contemporary jewellery is grouped into clusters. Works from different makers are arranged in groups of five or six, and each group throws light on a type of creative system or kind of social thinking. The works talk to each other as if in conversation, held together as much by their differences as by their family resemblances.

Built on a curiosity about ways of thinking and seeing, I have long sought to understand how jewellery, as a craft, has been overlaid with perspectives from art and design. Individual pieces can be approached in a variety of ways—in terms of rarified art or seductive design. All are craft and convey the interests of jewellers who take immense pleasure in making. More than anything, I hope that *Unexpected Pleasures* highlights jewellery's great capacity to absorb many layers of meaning when it speaks for different people. Perhaps this versatility is what separates contemporary jewellery from other types of cultural objects and makes it such a compelling case for exploring the relationships between art, craft and design.

Making

When pursuing an object of desire, which would you prefer: something that is beautifully made but doesn't really work, or something that is wonderfully conceived despite being poorly executed? This isn't always a clear choice: good design and good making each involve a skilled resolution between aesthetics and function. But jewellery is made to adorn and has no obvious utility. So how does contemporary jewellery work as a status signifier, and how do design approaches fit within the making experience?

The pleasure of making lies in playing with source materials to bring an idea to life. This involves working through the unknown. There is the tension between conceiving an idea, applying the right process and improvising to materialise an object. There is the potential in this for real headaches. You cannot always rely on your knowledge or past experiences alone. Thinking will often need to be undone as a way to discover different approaches, and here lies the pleasure.

First comes the idea for an object. Will the piece provide the opportunity for me to make a comment, hone a technique or exploit a material? A range of considerations are then set out and addressed, either in tandem or succession. Many makers are led by the object's physicality—decisions about materials, scale, texture and form. Some extend this into considering how the piece should be worn on the body. Where will it sit? How will it stay there? What will these choices mean for different wearers? Will I make the jewellery openly accessible or target it to a particular audience or wearer?

The finished pieces reveal a lot about makers' processes and intentions. It may be readily apparent that the maker envisions the object as belonging to a recognisable sensory language. Try to decipher the maker's design approach by checking the tactility of the object's surface, its graphic character and its relation to the space that it occupies. Ask yourself what its emotional and cultural values are. As Deyan Sudjic writes in *The Language of Things,* design engages through the sense "that there is something to understand about objects beyond the obvious issues of function and purpose".[3] Aesthetics are not merely about visual character but an experience that takes in all the senses. That is to say, aesthetics concern the object's relationship to people. This can also give some indication as to the level at which the maker absorbs design thinking into making.

Sudjic goes on, "there is much to be gained from exploring what objects mean as from considering what they do and what they look like".[4] This is as true for a contemporary jeweller as it is for the designers and users of a typeface, a chair or a software application. But sensitivity to design language is not always to be found in the foreground when viewing or handling contemporary jewellery works. Often jewellers concentrate their creative strategies within the activities of making. Materials, especially, will always impose their own demands. Jewellers have a unique understanding about the character of different materials, including how they will react through making processes.

Creative strategies evolve over time. Makers draw on an accumulated body of knowledge, skill and tactics. There is no ideal how-to because no method is the only way of making. You are guided by your own expectations and discoveries, which can open new considerations, pose new problems and reveal next steps.

I am constantly bemused, when telling someone I am a jeweller, to be asked, "Could you fix my watch?" I cannot. I can design how it will look, fix the watch to a chain, and imprint a jeweller's understanding of its relation to the body. But the internal mechanisms will never be my domain. They demand a special set of skills and training more familiar to makers of a kindred trade. Nonetheless, the watchmaker and I both make small things that are precious because they hold time. Jewellery's status as a luxury object has always related to the time, skill and effort that goes into its making. In traditional jewellery, time is invested to properly realise the value of material perceived to be precious because it is scarce or just costly.

So does making provide one key to understanding preciousness in jewellery? In my own experience, skill tends to assume an almost dictatorial influence when people seek to express the value they see in a contemporary jewellery work. Skill asserts its hegemony in a simple utterance: "Isn't it beautiful!" But in modern times, beauty (which is often said to be timeless) is always suspect, distracting us from the values, flaws and subterfuge buried beneath illustrious surfaces.

Mass production used to be seen as the other to making. Sudjic observes that "we used to know what mass production looked like, and what was handmade".[5] The concept of good design initially referred to an exclusive high-culture object. Well-designed objects, reflecting high craft ideals but made democratic through design processes, were used to signify good lifestyle and social status. As the art writer Terry Smith observes, in place of traditional craft cultures society erected designed systems for efficiently managing production and distribution. The makers were alienated from their audience, or so it goes. But has the emphasis on usability in contemporary design restored this relationship within industrial systems?[6]

Even societies dominated by industrial approaches need craft culture. In industry, making skills are distributed across large networks of people engaged with technology-based manufacture. This does suggest that making might at least endure as a residual practice in industrial design, though this would be a quite different concept of making than the one advanced by most contemporary jewellers.

Good design also taps strongly into popular imagination. Since the concept gained currency, it has been proven time and time again that well-designed objects have an innate power to provoke speculations and dreams that reflect our changing habits and lifestyles, so the concept of good design has come to impact across cultures and industries. Today good design is pervasive, even integral. And our possessions appear increasingly precious less for their material value or utility than for the emotional experiences they offer us—experiences that are widely accessible and through which we seek belonging.

In the 1980s, my sense that I belonged as a maker in the Contemporary Jewellery Movement came down to two things: its resistance against the mainstream and its modernist spirit. I felt that this challenge against traditional expectations in jewellery—particularly against its elite status and preciousness—fitted with my interest in design's possibilities. *Linking Links* shows the many different ways that contemporary jewellers fold design processes into making. But I recognise that my deliberate embrace of industrial processes has always placed me at the periphery of the movement. This is obvious, first and foremost, in the way my work responds to other makers', second, in the way that I talk about works, and third, in the thinking that has gone into *Unexpected Pleasures*.

→ 156

Other makers have positioned themselves over the years in other distinctive ways—through teaching, performance, photography, public discussions and private conversations. Most importantly, makers establish their positions through making. This is not to say that the clustering of works in *Linking Links* represent differences in makers' personalities. Rather, clusters offer examples of how works speak to one another, and by doing so they position their makers across a set of creative systems that define what contemporary jewellery means over time. Creative strategies and design processes must be viewed as tactics sometimes shared; they are a dialogue between many about making, about jewellery, and about the ever-changing worlds in which contemporary jewellery operates.

For contemporary jewellers the creative systems that define what we do are imprinted in the experiences of making. No matter how visceral the improvisations, or how far we are led to discover new approaches, the creative systems by which we work compel us again and again to reoccupy a favorite starting point or draw inspiration from others working across the same creative landscape. In these ways, creative systems can guide us to more effectively manage our time.

ABOVE · Ted Noten · *Chew Your Own Brooch* · 1998 · Brooch · Chewing gum · 70 × 10 × 3 mm

RIGHT · Ted Noten · *Chew Your Own Brooch* · 1998 · Brooch · Gold-plated silver · Various sizes

OPPOSITE · Manon van Kouswijk · *Paper Pearls* · 2001 · Neck piece · Cotton, archive stickers · Necklaces 350 mm, stickers 8 mm

SEE MORE of the **LOGICAL SOLUTIONS** cluster → **158**

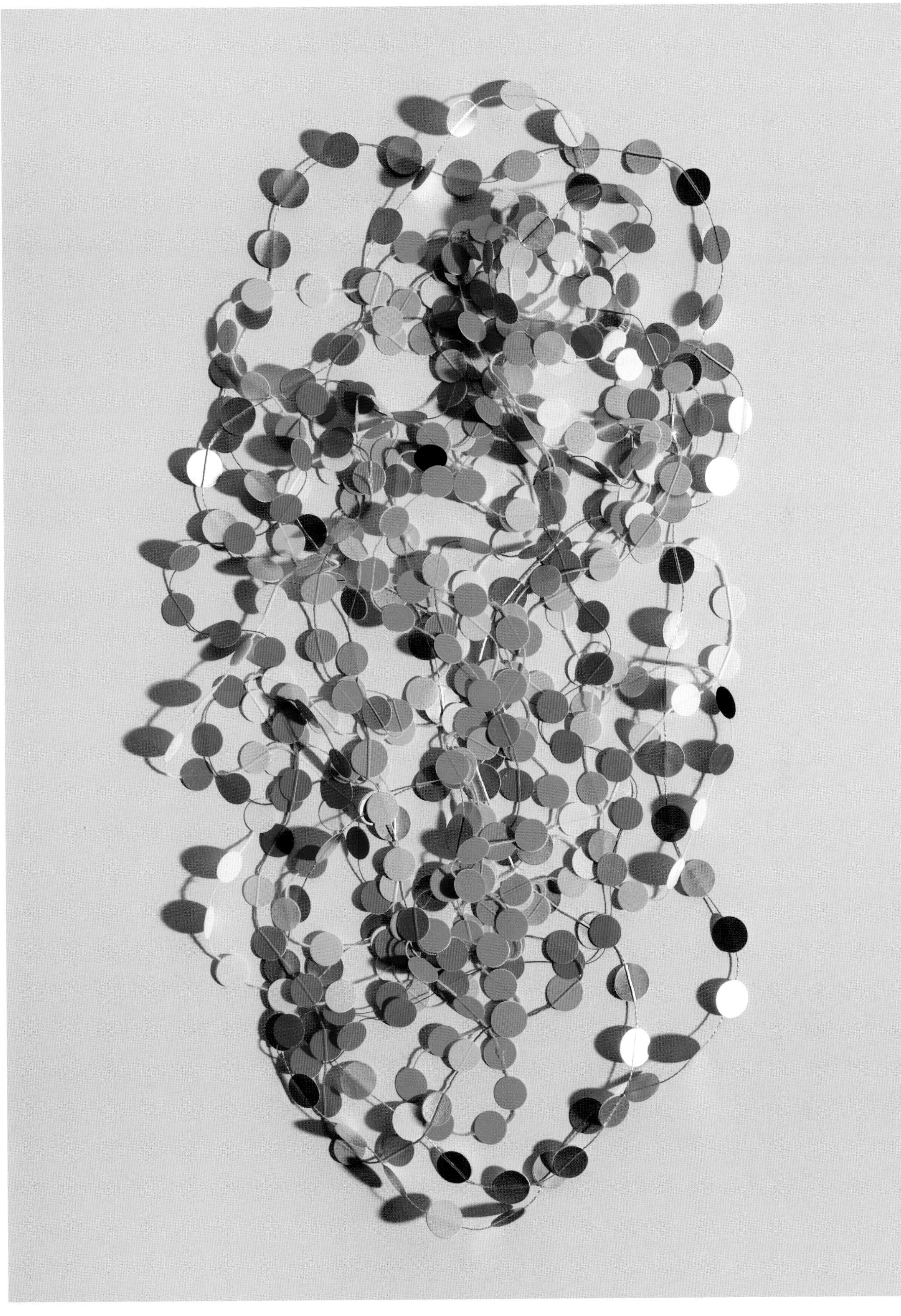

Certain makers play with systems to produce multiple objects. Contemporary jewellery has always tended to differentiate itself through its alignment with art, and it has been seduced by the allure of the original object. It seems there is now a widening stream of jewellers who recognise that design approaches offer *Logical Solutions* for reproducing original work. → 158 This would seem to provide a natural entry point for understanding where making belongs in design and where design occurs within making.

When adapted into jewellery practice, industrial materials and processes can be used to produce standardised elements that are easily reproduced. Makers will sometimes mirror and extend industrial-design systems to produce multiple originals. In some cases, this involves adapting a ready-made product such as the snap fastener or bike chain. The maker will exploit the repetition in elements that allows these objects to be mass-produced.

Repetition provides a starting point for simple making or craft-based experimentation, with the aim to produce unique luxury objects. In turn, by introducing jewellery values into design, makers highlight how industrial products become an integral part of our everyday experiences. The wearer may, for instance, be invited to recombine standard elements to make their own original interpretations. Or they may be to assigned a role as designer in a move to limit the designer's role to that of a skilled maker.

The aesthetic qualities of a design object offer pleasure. Part of the pleasure is in how the object contains little differences that appeal to many senses, even when those differences are made at scale through mass production. Contemporary jewellers who make *Multiple Originals* seek this diversity within works and through the relationships between works in a series. → 160

Perhaps this is why contemporary jewellers frequently return to natural forms. Craft writer David Pye observes that in this contemporary age hand making is understood to exploit diversity in a way that is "akin to the natural environment that we have abandoned".[7] The connection is especially important for makers who adorn—people have always worn out nature, from gemstones to wreaths of thorns.

Working with jewellery requires a focus on the micro scale. Once a logical solution for reproducing work is found, the flow in making can detain you; you keep uncovering minor variations on a single theme. The making unites dexterity with imaginative response, enabling long-term excursions through difference. For makers engaged with industrial processes this can provide points where craftsmanship ends and ordinary manufacture begins.[8] But it can also take you beyond a domain controlled by design. With each multiple original you extract new form, creating balance through symmetry, always with an acute awareness of the object's perimeter.

ABOVE · **Sue Lorraine** · *Petal Brooches* · 2000–2011 · Brooch · Heat-coloured mild steel, stainless-steel pins · 50 mm diameter
SEE MORE of the **LOGICAL SOLUTIONS** cluster → 158

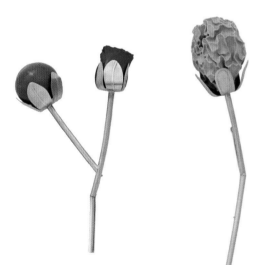

TOP · **Sally Marsland** · *Flat Colour* · 2002 ·
Brooch · Epoxy resin mixed with powdered pigment · 45 × 45 × 8 mm

MIDDLE · **Esther Knobel** · *Variations on a Rose* · 1991 ·
Brooch · Copper, nickel, silver, dried roses, dried fruit, chewing gum · 110 × 20 mm

BOTTOM · **Marian Hosking** · *Shell Shard Rings* · 2005 ·
Ring · Shell shard, .925 silver · 28 × 22 × 30 mm diameter (approx.)

SEE MORE of the **MULTIPLE ORIGINALS** cluster → **160**

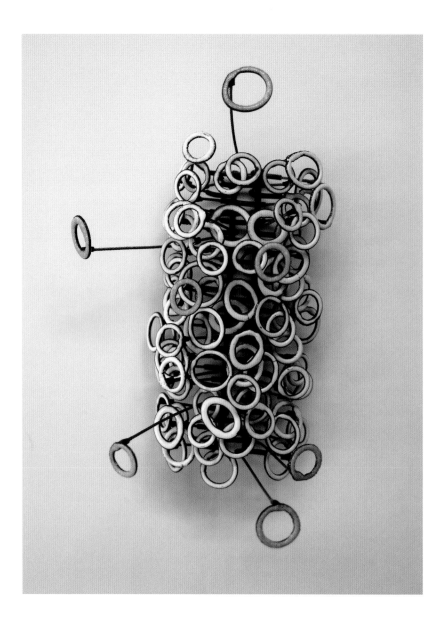

→ 162 Works in the *Negative Space* cluster place emphasis on the relationship between the object and the space that it occupies. The significance of form is practically offset by the sense of what is not there. This negative force exerts an equal positive charge.

Some contemporary jewellery works that play with negative space remind me of architectural forms. As individual works they may have a design logic that extends across a series, but each is independent in its solution. Just as the experience of a building cannot be separated from the cityscape on which it sits—and each work here comes from a different culture—you can imagine the character of these works could be enhanced in unexpected ways when worn on different bodies.

OPPOSITE · **Susie Ganch** · *Yellow Dust* · 2010 ·

Brooch · Enamelled copper, sterling silver, stainless steel · 106 × 60 × 65 mm

TOP · **Fabrizio Tridenti** · *Untitled* · 2010 ·

Brooch · Silver, brass, acrylic paint, iron · 75 × 107 × 34 mm

BOTTOM · **Jiro Kamata** · *Momentopia* · 2009 ·

Brooch · Camera lenses, acrylic paint, oxidised silver · 60 × 60 × 10 mm

SEE MORE of the **NEGATIVE SPACE** cluster → **162**

For this maker, there's a great attraction in the idea of working through these possibilities. Jewellery making has always been a matter of handling with care. Traditionally this was in the name of releasing the intrinsic value of precious materials. While contemporary jewellers shift the commercial basis for the object, it is always easy when handling materials to become seduced. Material qualities speak to you. They can trigger overpowering sensations. Every maker → 164 knows it: the *Physical Matters*.

ABOVE RIGHT · John Iversen · *Cracked Up* · 2009 · Brooch · Sterling silver, 750 yellow gold · 89 mm diameter

ABOVE LEFT · Helen Britton · *Nighttime* · 2009 · Brooch · Silver, paint, glass · 100 × 90 × 70 mm

SEE MORE of the **PHYSICAL MATTERS** cluster → 164

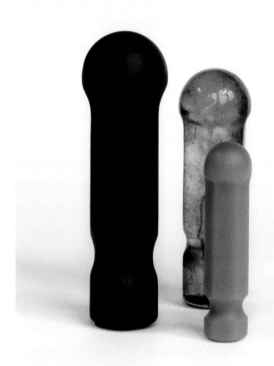

ABOVE RIGHT · **Yutaka Minegishi** · *Whipped Cream* · 2010 ·
Ring · Mammoth bone · 38 × 30 × 30 mm

ABOVE LEFT · **Yutaka Minegishi** · *Hidden Rips* · 2010 ·
Ring · Ebony · 40 × 32 × 27 mm

SEE MORE of the **HAND MADE** cluster → **166**

LEFT · **Warwick Freeman** · *Handle Pendants* · 2008 ·
Pendants · Jet, kauri gum, jade · Various sizes: Jet handle 105 × 30 mm

SEE MORE of the **PHYSICAL MATTERS** cluster → **164**

→ 166

Form, materials, negative space: each has its own allure. These seductions mingle together in the stimulation that comes when jewellery is *Handmade*.

Hand making can sometimes feel like alchemy. You gain rare insight and appreciation for how this precious jewellery stuff works. You become deeply involved with its idea at a most intimate, tactile level. Though doubts may sometimes enter and limit your ability to perform, it's an electric feeling when you round every base. Perhaps this explains many jewellers' reluctance to defer to design approaches. The addiction says, don't give up the high that comes with real-time thinking—don't let design impose its order on things.

The feeling is exacerbated by the sense that those who handle your goods can sense your meditations, knowing the piece is handmade.

Machine making requires an equal state of connection between mind and object. Everything is eliminated but the task itself. You must rely on both natural intuition and inherited skill. But the handmade means made with love. Receiving an artisan object can feel like a deeply personal invitation to connect with skilled traditions, and these traditions are what bind a community that makes meaning through making. So when you receive a handmade object, you are asked to share in this communal bond, between maker and giver.

ABOVE · **Nel Linssen** · *Bracelet* · 2008 ·
Bracelet · Plastic-covered paper · section 85 mm × height 20 mm
OPPOSITE · **Gabriela Horvat** · *Fabulas Rurales* · 2011 ·
Neck piece · .925 silver, wool, silk, copper, steel · 1,500 × 250 × 100 mm
SEE MORE of the **HANDMADE** cluster → **166**

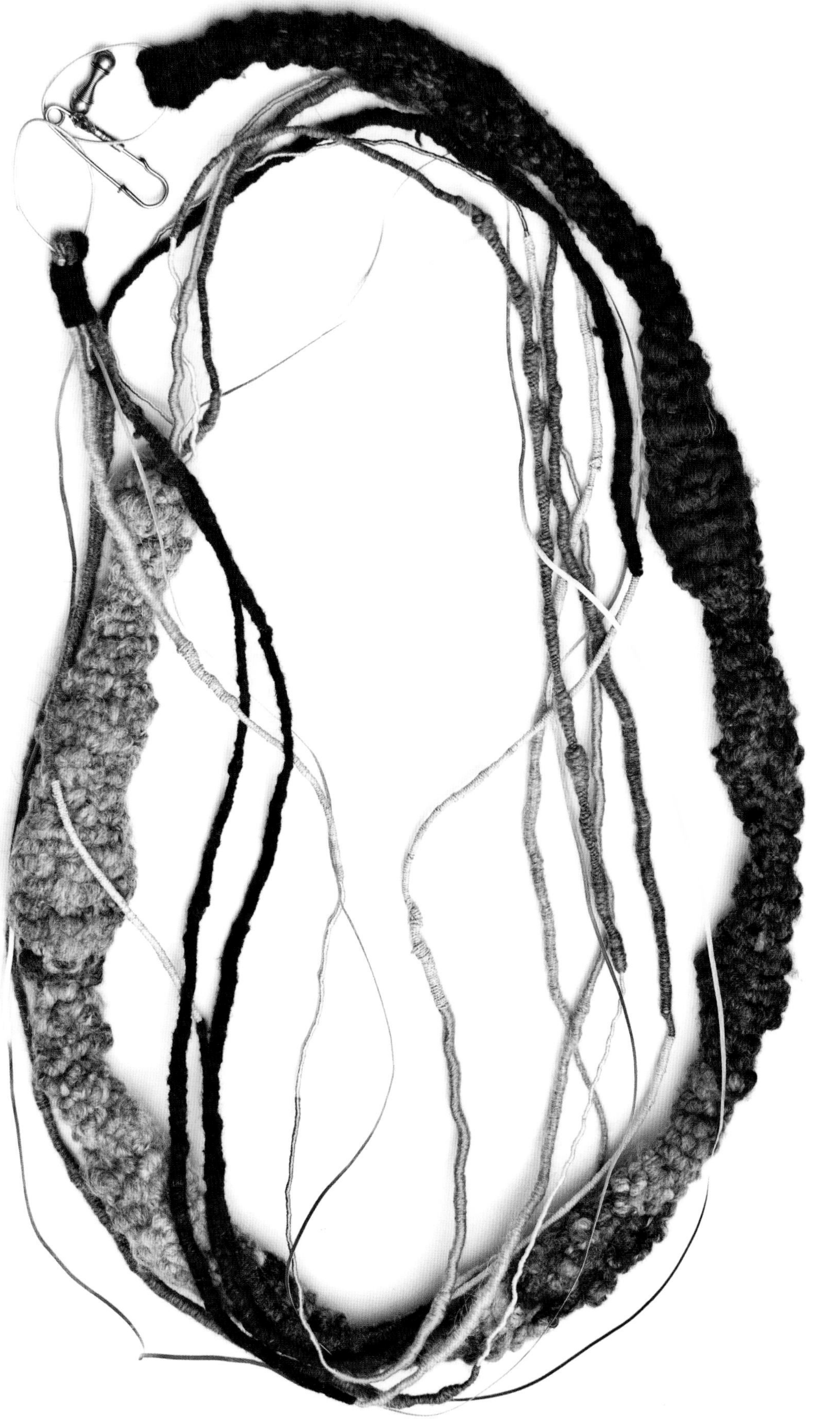

Such emotional resonance is often stated in response to aesthetics. Something made by hand, it is said, is just more beautiful than a machine-made object. Jewellers may take a cruel pleasure in this notion: jewellery can be made beautiful through its use because it takes on the aesthetics of its wearer. The connections that a wearer gives to jewellery can blind them to its beauty, or lack thereof. There is in this a space to play, and it is not rare for contemporary jewellers to seduce people through hand making only to position them through jewellery ideas in unexpected ways.

Contemporary jewellers have always understood that hand signature in making can be used to articulate a perspective on the world and contemporary jewellery's place within it. When looking at the works of long-standing players, what may seem like *Quirky Ideas* are often the effective means by which a maker maps contemporary jewellery's values and boundaries.

→ 168

Each jewellery piece in the *Quirky Ideas* cluster is the work of an important contemporary jewellery maker and reflects the distinctive personas that these makers have achieved through a prolonged engagement with their making. Over time, adept skill and handling creates difference. The I gradually appears across a series of works. So signature can be said to extend naturally out of the attractions in making.

Maturity in aesthetics suggests both skill and a highly developed sense of artistic purpose. For leaders in the field this can equate to a coherent artistic identity that can be traded on for influence and authority—say, when teaching others in the craft. At the same time, with signature works there is often something unexpected in the idea—perhaps an idiosyncratic approach to jewellery. You may see how strongly the influencers in contemporary jewellery have been influenced by aesthetics in art. It is not necessarily something about the styles, per se; it is more in the way these works open questions about the source for ideas in the field.

The push by jewellers to establish signature in making has a basis in commercial trade, but gained real momentum within the Contemporary Jewellery Movement. It emerged precisely on the cusp between modernism and postmodernism, and this has had a continuing influence on how different groups of makers fold in outside influences. Makers who have not fully embraced postmodernism's abandon, but who have sought artistic identity through hand making, tend to trace the eccentric perimeters to the creative landscape they inhabit. Others situate their practice in connection to the movement's response to modernism's design aesthetic. And modernism was never just a style. For contemporary jewellers it was a unifying force that pushed out the limits to practice and opened possibilities that went beyond just jewellery.

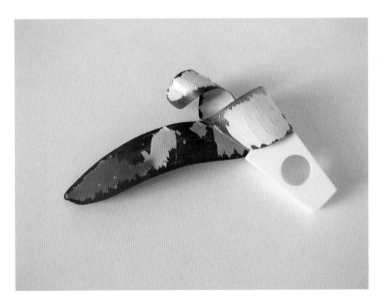

OPPOSITE · **Georg Dobler** · *Dragonfly Beetle* · 2008 ·
Brooch · Oxidised silver, citrine · 145 × 90 × 18 mm
ABOVE · **Ruudt Peters** · *Lingam Black* · 2010 ·
Pendant · Wood, glass, electoformed silver · 200 × 140 × 300 mm
RIGHT · **Fritz Maierhofer** · *Studio Ring 1* · 2011 ·
Ring · Corian, silver, gold, paper, paint · 110 × 120 × 35 mm
SEE MORE of the **QUIRKY IDEAS** cluster → **168**

A *Modernist Spirit* has continued to provide fluent pulse for a movement caught in a cultural slipstream. By the mid-1980s, at a time when the Contemporary Jewellery Movement was reaching its heights, conservative critics like Christopher Lasch were lamenting the psychological and social impacts of a then-emerging consumer culture. In Lasch's view, the rise of an information age meant a world obsessed with celebrity, youthfulness and material "things". Lasch's charge was that such a culture negates the potential for introspection or substantive inner life.[9] This notion would appear to resonate strongly today for those who fear the overwhelming impacts of networked computing on community life.

ABOVE · **Beppe Kessler** · *Timeless* · 2008 · Brooch · Silver, soapstone, acrylic fiber, red cedar wood · 60 × 60 × 20 mm

OPPOSITE TOP · **Warwick Freeman** · *Lattice* · 1994 · Brooch · Cow bone · 67 × 67 mm

OPPOSITE BOTTOM · **Mark Edgoose** · *Ring and Box No.1* · 2010 · Ring · Niobium · 30 × 30 × 25 mm diameter

SEE MORE of the **MODERNIST SPIRIT** cluster → 170

But—especially—in an age of narcissism, jewellery retains power as a visible token of affection and intimate investment. And makers continue to put creative systems to work in the name of unexpected pleasures. Some jewellers continue to develop a signature using modernism's stripped-back aesthetics, asserting a potent continuity between past values and → 172 contemporary poetic forms. Others adopt an *Anything Goes* mentality, finding difference in work through a serious attention to play. Sidestepping the refined elegance and concentrated emotion that runs through modernist forms, they pitch for easy wonderment. Celebrating colour, plasticisty and soft ties, they feed handmade jewellery signs back into a culture in overdrive and invite us to play in the game.

Recycling has almost become mainstream as a mantra in developed societies. Wasted and discarded objects form the background to our lives. Time seems to be measured in the short life cycle or unexpected durability of the objects we use, own and all too frequently replace. In making there is the potential to restore, resurrect and reinvent the detritus of fast living.

TOP · **Maud Traon** · *The Agony of the Narrative* · 2011 · Ring · Foam putty, found object, varnish · 35 × 60 × 35 mm

BOTTOM · **Adam Paxon** · *Brooch with Four Eyes* · 2009 · Brooch · Acrylic, lacquer, enamel · 70 × 100 × 100 mm

OPPOSITE · **Noon Passama** · *Angel Hair* · 2010 · Brooch · Fur, 14k gold-plated brass, polyester filling, remanium · 30 × 90 × 47 mm diameter

SEE MORE of the **ANYTHING GOES** cluster → 172

Many contemporary jewellers like to reflect on current concerns and encourage comment through work. Materials may be found, rather than sourced, and this alone amounts to an important statement: it's what we salvage that must become the new precious. In my own view, the works in *Second Life* seem to suggest that there is a currency in rethinking how we care for our environment. It's not just the materials: the ideas are fun, and the elements are commonplace—ice-cream containers, milk bottles, construction materials, debris that has washed up on the shore. So many people can enjoy these works—that is to say, by the everyday language of the objects salvaged the works take on a natural democratic appeal.

→ 174

Speculating on the intentions of the maker you can draw a deeper thread, a call to makers and an invitation to wearers: new and inventive approaches to identity and belonging may just be exactly what we need to collectively push for change. Resolving an idea that has real currency can mean liberating the timeless function of jewellery as a force for belonging.

Currency in work can also be expressed by aesthetics achieved using new technologies. It is not only makers in the emerging generation of jewellers but also some with strong backgrounds in hand making who are now exploring the potential to achieve new jewellery styles through digital production. In one sense, this challenges the traditional centrality of hand making in jewellery craft. By another logic, there is a natural attraction for skilled jewellers to open up possibilities in making by mastering the aesthetics of our time. With computers and production software now in every home and mobile on the streets, creative systems have fallen out of the trained hands of an elite and into the dexterous hands of many. We are more sympathetic to the idea that design process and reproduction relies on intuitive skill, backed by creative ideas and responsive thinking. In fact, for many of us—whether we're listening to electronic music, hunting street stencil work or wearing out contemporary jewellery—there is an undeniable attraction to artists who take a no-hands approach to signature. Their art seems to beckon *Finish Me Off* inviting audiences into a productive relationship and giving us an active role in the making process.

→ 176

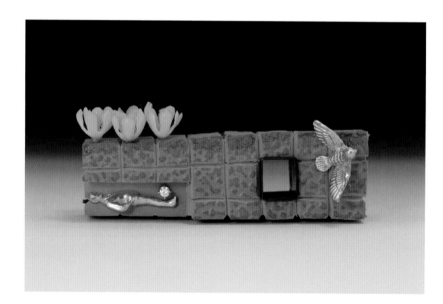

ABOVE · Taweesak Molsawat · *This is Thai: Article No. 1 08-14-2009* · 2010 · Brooch · Sterling silver, copper, used plastic, floating used EVA foam, CZ · 25 × 85 × 22 mm
OPPOSITE TOP · Sally Marsland · *Odd One Out* · 2010 · Pendant · Wood, paint · 70 × 40 × 40 mm
OPPOSITE BOTTOM · Karl Fritsch · *Screw Ring* · 2010 · Ring · Silver, nails, screws · 60 × 40 × 40 mm
SEE MORE of the **SECOND LIFE** cluster → 174

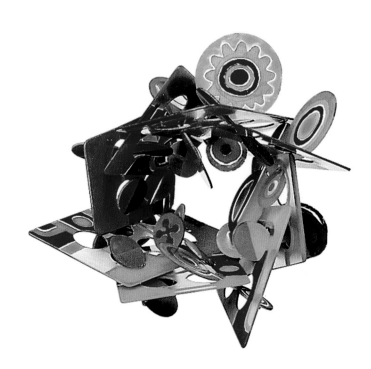

ABOVE LEFT · **Gijs Bakker** · *Porsche* · 2002 · Bracelet · Polyurethane · 34 × 75 × 98 mm · Made by Chi ha paura…?

ABOVE RIGHT · **Svenja John** · *Bugi Bracelet* · 1996 · Bracelet · Polycarbonate · 70 × 80 × 80 mm

OPPOSITE · **David Watkins** · *Sleeper's Thicket 4* · 2009 · Bracelet · Acrylic, gold · 150 × 150 × 12 mm

SEE MORE of the **FINISH ME OFF** cluster → **176**

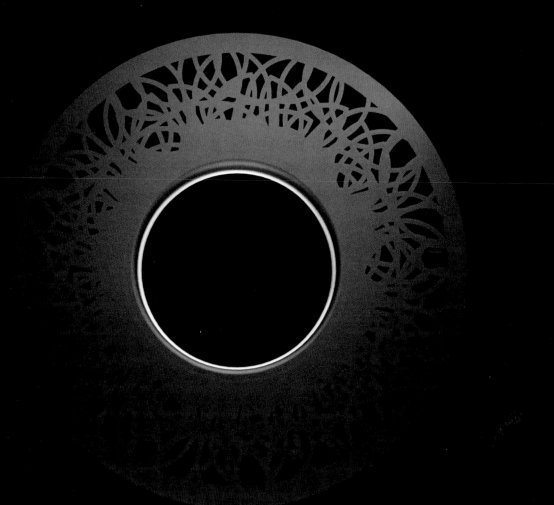

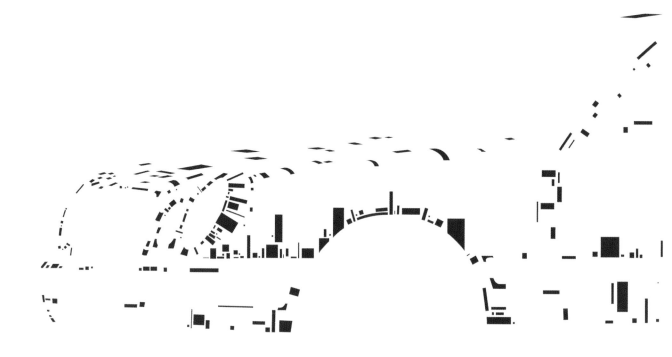

→ 178

The discussion so far has been on the seductions in making. We have traced back through the vibrant and colourul work of material revivalists to the modernist residues in poetic jewellery stylists. Hand making is important in defining the status of the object and how this status can be used to reinforce idea and challenged through the embrace of new technologies. What all these clusters point to are the many and diverse ways in which contemporary jewellers have engaged with design processes and thinking. Over the course of its history, the edges of contemporary jewellery have been staked out on the positions of makers with different *Industrial Views*. These may range from folding in design processes with an aim to accentuate the beauty in jewellery forms to fully embracing industrial products and processes. There are rare examples where makers have sampled from design's brand and product catalogue to heighten the jewellery's sense as a force for belonging. In turn, with products like the Apple iPod Shuffle, it is evident that industrial designers are adapting jewellery values back into commercial culture.

Though it has informed contemporary jewellery from its beginnings, the conversation with design offers jewellers a space for continued reinvention and outreach. Design operates on the basis that we all are open to being flattered by our possessions. And contemporary jewellers have an intuitive and inherited understanding that flattery begins in the pleasures of the maker. As a maker I sometimes wonder whether the seductions in making are so strong that design process trumps design thinking. The engagement is certainly complicated by contemporary jewellery's ongoing relationships to craft and art, which tend to reinforce the values of hand making and the original object. The works in *Unexpected Pleasures* demonstrate that contemporary jewellers approach design from a range of directions, and this includes both engaging with the emotional language of design objects and critically assessing its impacts through jewellery ideas. Design encourages us to think about the end user, and in jewellery's case this is the wearer. Attuning our thinking and making to the pleasures of the wearer will allow makers to produce jewellery that is truly relevant and contemporary to our times.

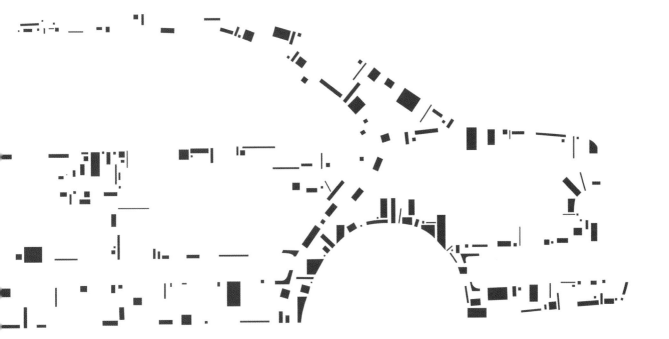

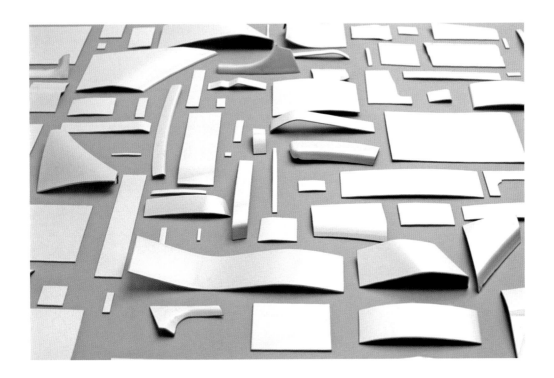

TOP · **Ted Noten** · *Mercedes-Benz E-classe 210* · 2001 ·
Photograph · Photograph printed on aluminium, acrylic covering · 600 × 1,600 × 30 mm

ABOVE · **Ted Noten** · *Mercedes-Benz E-classe 210* · 2003 ·
Brooch · Mercedes-Benz car body · Various sizes

SEE MORE of the **INDUSTRIAL VIEWS** cluster → **178**

Wearing

Jewellery attains status as a symbol for belonging, and its emotional values form in response to the many occasions when jewellery is worn out. For contemporary jewellers, imagining different ways to fashion the body offers foundations for art and design practice. The creative process begins in the making, continues through the photographing and exhibiting of works, and perhaps most essentially extends through the experiences of collecting and wearing. While fashion seduces us by design, contemporary jewellery maintains a more direct relationship to its wearers, a relationship bounded by the mutual recognition of certain art and craft values.

Jewellery presupposes the body. Rings, bracelets, anklets, neck rings, chokers, tiaras and chains are circles that wrap around our fingers, wrists, ankles, heads and necks. Earrings clip onto our ears, brooches are pinned to strategic positions on the front torso, and pendants swing in time to our movements. We use jewellery to draw attention to specific zones for personal and cultural reasons. Playing with jewellery can make us more conscious about how we use our bodies to communicate or to settle. Jewellery habits can also be unconscious, allowing worn objects to infiltrate our body image over time.

Jewellery falls under dress. Along with our clothing, sunglasses and wearable technologies it serves as a public sign of our being in the world. Maurice Merleau-Ponty observes that without calculation a woman may feel where a feather in her hat ends and keep a safe distance from things that might break it off.[11] In the same way, wearing a ring can become so deeply ingrained that removing it will induce a phantom memory—an experience that resonates out through the body leaving you feeling mildly unstable.

In 1973, Gijs Bakker produced a remarkable series of images. They were designed to show that when jewellery is removed, the "physical form of the jewel disappears" but not the imposition of its idea.[12] Bakker wrapped gold wire around various body zones and then removed it, employing photography as a device to capture the marks on the body, which he called Shadow Jewellery (Schaduwsieraad). It was an artistic statement, articulating his challenge against jewellery's expected pleasures—the notion that jewellery's preciousness resides in its form. Even today it is a challenging work. Many wearers appreciate the anything-goes mentality in contemporary jewellery but still identify value as belonging in the aesthetics and aura of hand craftsmanship. Likewise, many makers who find jewellery's seductions in the making—the tango with materials, form and process—would judge Shadow Jewellery still to be a disruptive work.

Contemporary makers have long viewed the body as a subject for artistic expression. Emmy van Leersum, Peter Skubic, Otto Künzli and other makers from the Contemporary Jewellery Movement sought to bring attention back to the body. Their ideas and motives varied, but there is a unifying thread: jewellery has a unique relationship to the body, and in this relationshop there are clues to how jewellery distinguishes itself as an item of dress.

Thinking about Bakker's historical work I have always been struck with how it mimics the terms of jewellery's natural life. If you take off a wedding ring to signal your availability, the skin underneath where the ring has been can be so soft that any astute interested party will infer the truth. For the wearer, guilt about indiscretions may haunt through the phantom memory of the absent ring. And if you're really attuned to how the wedding ring works, its codes can even be twisted to advantage. You might stage the revelation of a marked finger as an intended sign that your lover should expect only unexpected pleasures. As Bakker says, jewellery's physical form is just the "wrapping of an idea" that leaves its impression on the wearer.[13]

Peter Dormer has suggested that contemporary jewellers have used the body to reclaim jewellery as art.[14] In thinking through Unexpected Pleasures I have considered this proposition. I am curious, especially, in how contemporary jewellers fashion the body using photography, and how this might suggest an ongoing conversation across those fine lines between art, craft and design.

In some respects, contemporary jewellery operates on the same basis as fashion. Fashion nourishes itself through its own reincarnations. Fashion designers work across a set of creative systems, staking out positions relating to workmanship, materials, value and aesthetics. They fold in design approaches and industrial systems, engaging in a focused sampling from across cultures, with few fixed rules. As in art jewellery, luxury status is assigned through the maker's signature. And makers speak through their designs, articulating fresh perspectives about the world and where their shared creative space sits within. Just as the clusters in Unexpected Pleasures represent conversations between makers, artistry in fashion produces works that speak about fashion. The conversation within the field then provides the basis for widespread commercialisation. The artistry present in the work informs the wearer's experience, its status emanating through the feeling that comes when dressed in style.

Ordinary clothing can be utilitarian in appeal. Jackets keep us warm, shoes ensure our protection, and uniforms authorise access to certain zones and spaces. Fashion can disrupt this with artistic intent. "Of the moment" style (which can be traditional, retro or futuristic) is elevated as priority number one. Designers will often take unwearability as an artistic force and innovative impulse.

→ 116

There's a kind of frivolousness, and gravity also, in wearing fashion out. Even though ordinary jewellery has no obvious function, contemporary jewellers play for the same taste distinctions. The *Worn Out* section includes photographs featuring some of the most uninhibited works and identities in the field. Makers, you may notice, can also push the limits when it comes to jewellery's wearability. If you're ever lucky enough to wear one of these borderline-fashion pieces, you may be struck at how strongly wearing is considered in making. These pieces can quickly rebalance your embodied experience and reorient your relation to others in a room.

Contemporary jewellers strive to invent luxury objects and influential images. We are always sampling ideas and looks from the worlds around us, and as in fashion the status of work is linked to artistic intent. Some jewellers seek to recast jewellery's relationship to different cultures of the body. An image might isolate a stomach, focusing your gaze on an intervention by jewellery. I am reminded of the urge with which people will modify their bodies to fashion themselves. Tattooing, piercing or scarring the body, cosmetic enhancements or medical prostheses—there's always a cultural influence, drawn from the mainstream or some periphery. The body provides a potent site for experimentation.

In the 1980s photography entered contemporary jewellery as a pivotal documentary tool. In traditional art and trade, making began with detailed sketching and drawing. By the end of the 1980s, makers were visually representing work to close the making process. Bakker's *Shadow Jewellery* was so powerful partly because he anticipated this shift nearly a decade before. The image was not merely integral to the making in that series—it *was* the making. Today, as Dormer observes, contemporary jewellers commonly will adopt the body as background material, arranging it as an inanimate sculpture upon which their art might work.

How might these images influence the experiences of wearing jewellery? To answer this question, it is worth looking at how fashion operates, drawing on art, design and craft approaches.

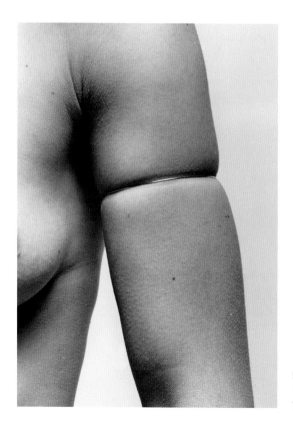

LEFT AND OPPOSITE · **Gijs Bakker** · *Shadow Jewellery* · 1973 ·
Photograph · Arm/waist pieces · Yellow-gold wire · 77 × 77 × 0.5 mm
This image is from **WORN OUT PHOTOGRAPHY: BODY → 146**

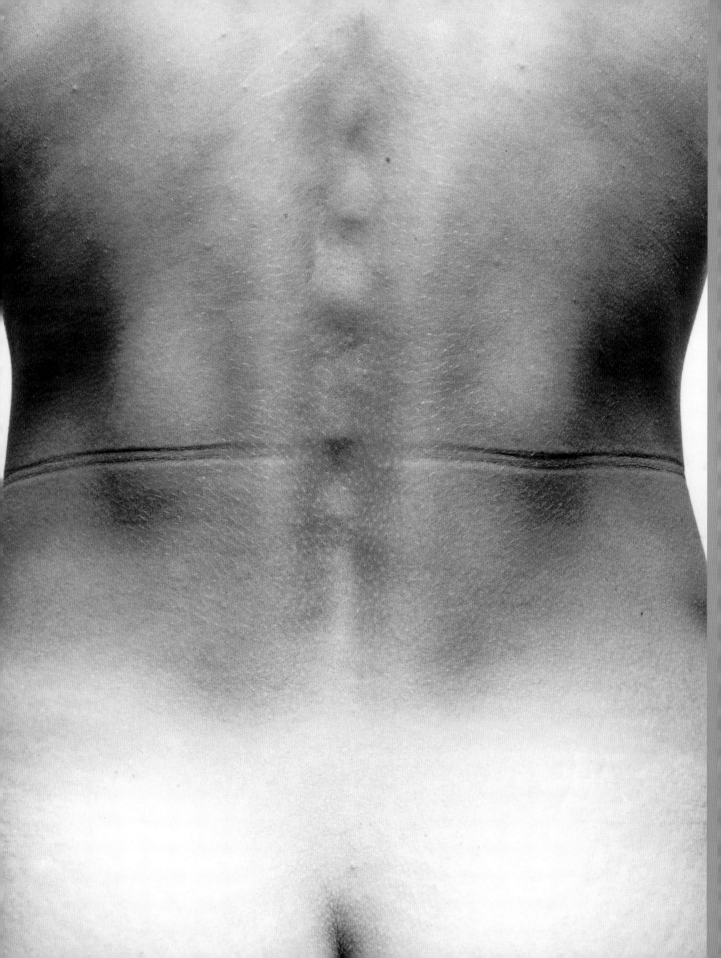

Fashion succeeds on the basis that it can deeply influence how we see ourselves through images. Image drives fashion's *trickle down*—a term that means nothing more than "haute couture ideas get mass produced", borrowing Dorothea Mink's phrasing.[15] Fashion achieves mass appeal and distribution through design approaches and systems. Design helps to turn the art-based "unreal" into a basis for commercial exploitation. The elite object is made democratic through mass manufacture, mass image and the machinations of mass culture. Deyan Sudjic tells us that fashion has "swallowed design whole", and it is through design's influence that fashion controls (to varying degrees of success) how we use dress and style for belonging.

As Mink writes, in a society where "the surface stands for content and pictures take the place of words, fashion offers us recognizable visual signs".[16] These are made all the more familiar because designers actively sample from culture's peripheries. The street tendencies brought forth by youth cultures bubble up into haute couture, feeding fashion's rapid and fickle cycles.

In this system images are essential—they have been so since the birth of modern fashion. Roland Barthes wrote in the 1960s about the image's role in "fashioning the body". For Barthes, fashion's influence on our idea of the body can be ordered into a progression. The body in its purest form gains definition through dress. Fashion intervenes by staging the body in various ways—on the catwalk, in magazine spreads, today across blogs assembled by dedicated followers. Every year we decree that a certain type of body is *in fashion*. The effect is to compromise the body's "pure structure". As a society of people we respond, developing dress to transform the real body and signify the ideal.[17]

OPPOSITE · **Caroline Broadhead** · *Veil* · 1983 ·

Photograph · Necklace/veil · Nylon · 300 × 300 × 300 mm · 600 × 300 × 300 mm

This image is from **WORN OUT ORIGINS → 130**

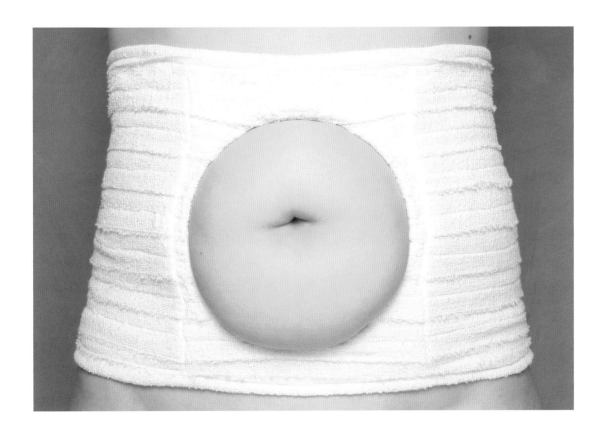

OPPOSITE · **Fran Allison** · *How to Make a Necklace from a Frock* · 2006 ·

Photograph · Necklace · Frock, fabric, silver, stainless-steel wire, lollipop sticks · Necklace: 630 × 300 × 80 mm

This image is from **WORN OUT PHOTOGRAPHY: JEWELLERY AS OBJECT → 138**

ABOVE · **Tiffany Parbs** · *Tuck* · 2008 · Photograph · Crepe bandage, digital print · 330 × 470 × 35 mm

This image is from **WORN OUT PHOTOGRAPHY: BODY → 146**

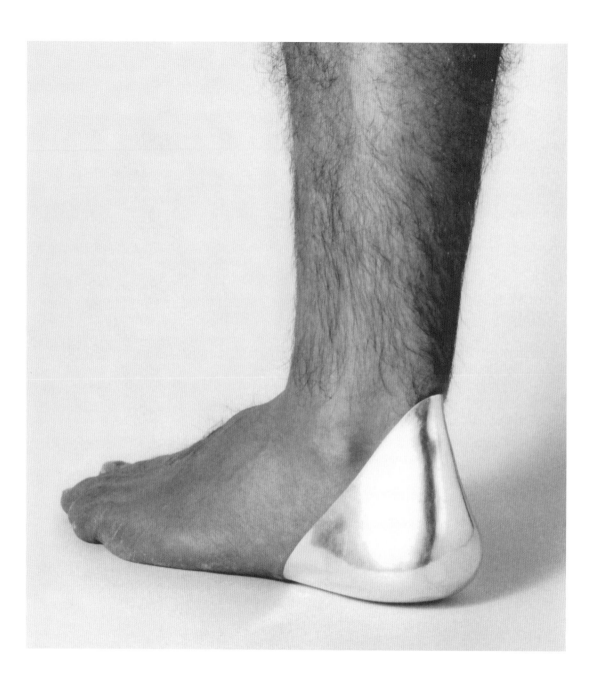

ABOVE · **Gerd Rothmann** · *Achilles' Heel* · 1978 · Photograph · Heel piece · Silver · 78 × 89 ×76 mm
This image is from **WORN OUT PHOTOGRAPHY: BODY → 146**

OPPOSITE · **Alexander Blank** · *Ed's Friend Rat* · 2009 · Photograph · Brooch · Rigid foam, silver, Perspex, lacquer · 65 × 47 × 115 mm
This image is from **WORN OUT PHOTOGRAPHY: JEWELLERY AS OBJECT → 138**

Fashion induces demand by playing on our natural instincts for imitation. Style in dress helps us to stand out, like Lady Gaga and her meat dress, to disappear, emulating Bob Dylan under his RayBans, or to position ourselves within a certain genre, just as Amy Winehouse used her beehive hairdo to channel 1960s soul. The fashion industry creates, revives and recombines images as contexts that allow us to easily read designs, brands and styles. As Barthes observes, fashion photography presents the world as décor, itself an aesthetic fantasy. The "unreal", born in the maker's artistry, turns "real" because the image mirrors and amplifies the world's sensory language. Everything within the frame, including the body, is stylised as part of an aesthetic fantasy, a poetic association between ideas, an easily deciphered code. The vision may begin with the maker, but it becomes democratic insofar as it offers an unattainable ideal that is accessible to all.

Jewellery is not the same as clothing. It operates by its own code, and it is differently implicated in the relationships we keep with others. It is charged as an accessory to our lives. Georg Simmel writes that an item of adornment can "single out its wearer", offering a kind of self-feeling that increases at the expense of others. But the pleasure in jewellery is also "designed for others", and the wearer derives enjoyment "only so far as he mirrors himself in them".[18]

Jewellery needs to be worn out to reach its potential as an intimate object, and its nuances will shift dramatically across contexts. Just look at the odd assortment of images in _Worn Out_. Together they reveal → 116 that jewellery propositions are rarely _just_ jewellery. These propositions rely on people. Some of the most ebullient works within this section are pictured within ordinary scenarios affixed to "real people", as if there was nothing unusual to see here. It's a tactic that's been employed since the 1980s, and it separates new jewellery from fashion. As opposed to a fantasy designed to aestheticise the real world, it is the elite artifact here that is drawn out of context. When you're absorbed within the image's frame, contemporary jewellery is removed from the gallery space, the private collection, the pictorial spread in the art book—all the first places you might look for it.

The effect is an inversion to fashion's commercial logic. Sure, there's still a fantasy at hand and a signature style at play. And yes, the image still says, "You want", dripping with high craft ideals, design thinking and art aesthetics. But the image seduces you with the individual pleasures of wearing. The luxury object is rendered "real" so it might respond like jewellery worn to your world.

OPPOSITE · **Rachel Timmins** · _I Want to Be a Gold Lobster with Blue Puffs_ · 2009 ·

Photography · Hand gloves · Found fabric, wool yarn, polyester stuffing, thread, copper, found gloves · 483 × 305 × 102 mm each

This image is from **WORN OUT: PHOTOGRAPHY→ 136**

Belonging

We are possessed by our belongings. They perform for us as we shape our worlds. Choose your lifestyle. Attract a partner. Consume commodities. Act out tastes. Fashion your body. Create your own distinctions. When jewellery adopts its wearer it is bestowed with the realities and fantasies of its new life. It becomes insinuated in the plots, stratagems and concealments of daily life. And, as your unreliable partner in crime, it talks.

At a time when societies were designing new languages for living, Barthes was attuned to jewellery's mythic heritage. His theory is inadequate, though, for understanding jewellery's social role because he neglects that we might be always inventing new ways to belong.

Belonging is an experience, a sense that you are a part of something. It is a promise that is traded through personal exchange and which drives community spirit. It is a feeling that might be shaped by a longing to be, or a decision about what you are not. You may be thinking that wherever I am I would not be better off somewhere else. Through all our worlds belonging is woven—a common thread with give. We are assembled by our differences as much as by our resemblances, bound by animal instincts and inessential features, crowning moments or forgotten tales, shared hearts or secrets held.

There is great artistry and freedom in how we express belonging. The pleasure in giving the right gift, for example, can be electric; a current that flows two ways, from the giver to the receiver and back outward through a circle of people connected to the exchange. A gift can be a present for a loved one, hospitality for friends or for a service rendered. Any of these may be driven by affection, obligation or some resolution between the two. When a woman sleeps with a man, she is said to give herself to him. There's a trade at play in giving, but rarely are you meant to keep score. It's more a simple pleasure: you recognise someone and in turn they recognise you.

We often express thinking about belonging when we engage in symbolic exchange. At a meeting in 1913, Sigmund Freud presented to each of the members in his professional inner circle an intaglio seal taken from his own antiquities collection. Before written signatures came into fashion, these ancient seals would have been used to certify documents. Freud's seals were mounted onto gold rings and worn by his circle as pledges of eternal union and allegiance to Freud, the ring giver.[19]

This episode, recounted in a book by Phyllis Grosskurth, offers us a way to think about jewellery as a gifted object. Jewellery can be fashioned to speak in intimate terms, and it takes on values given to it by many. In Freud's case, there would seem to be a potent connection between the seal, as an ancient form of signature, and the creative landscape that he and his followers inhabited. The founding psychoanalysts believed that our everyday expressions, incorporating language, objects and the body, surface unconscious drives and that these relate back to the foundational myths and structures of human society. The seals when fashioned as rings and given within a circle likely expressed an experience and concept of belonging peculiar to this group.

Perhaps there is always this kind of artistry in intimate exchange. Even the most personal givings are public in the sense that they coordinate us into giving circles that weave outward and expand and contract, interlocking along the way. The creative flash between a giver and a receiver is one of those elemental links by which our societies organise themselves. With each exchange we strike a new match that leads us working out not only where we belong, but also what belonging means to us.

Traditionally, a woman is given away when she is married, and as part of the pledge a ring might be passed down the inheritance line. Today, giving remains equally regimented—on top of traditions we have massive mercantile systems geared to stimulate giving in waves. Commerce aligns with tradition to dictate when we spend and how much, though this must always defer to our inventive spirit if a gift is to be genuine. In business, a true gift can inject real engagement into an essentially industrious relationship. By the same token, sales and giveaways will have limited effect if the company doesn't already hold an authentic connection with its community of consumers.

This is where design now intervenes. It offers us a symbolic language for belonging that is intuitive, culturally grounded and responsive to change. As Sudjic reminds us, design doesn't just shape the objects that possess us, it provides sensory clues about the object's function and values. The role of the designer today is as much to be a story teller as it is to resolve formal and functional problems, and the seduction is in how design's stories will speak for you.

Design communicates about belonging because it invents and elaborates upon certain archetypes for living. For example, a design object may be adopted on the street because it suggests the mystique of the outsider. Bruce Sterling observes that when cyberpunk fiction became a basis for a subculture in the 1980s, the group's members adopted mirrorshades sunglasses as totemic wear:

"mirrorshades prevent the forces of normalcy from realizing that one is crazed and possibly dangerous. They are the symbol of the sun-staring visionary, the biker, the rocker, the policeman and similar outlaws."[15]

For a Cyberpunk, these shades might feel like they cast you in an aesthetic fantasy founded in fiction but elaborated onto the world at large. Like any good story, the fantasy should accommodate differences in character, vision and outlook. Most essentially, the boundaries are set up against a mainstream. The Cyberpunks aggressively mirrored belonging on the "outside". Using design language they asserted an exclusive world vision, bordered off with danger signs marked up in a clear and common language.

Contemporary jewellers voice ideas about belonging through the objects they make. These ideas are founded in a shared creative landscape that reaches beyond the group. In *Unexpected Pleasures*, the → 156 *Linking Links* section presents a stream of works that are clustered to represent different kinds of social thinking. Jewellers play with widely recognised symbols, and on first glance they may seem to approaching something like a universal language for belonging.

Makers might, for instance, play on the *Heart Felt* feelings assumed to pulsate through all human relationships. As a recognised symbol for belonging, the heart stands out. And there is a resonance in seeing it used as a symbol for jewellery. Through making, jewellers can offer us inventive ways to voice our own hearts, to measure how easily we give them away and to show they've turned black when a loved one is lost. → 188

ABOVE · **Constanze Schreiber** · *Mourning I* · 2006 · Brooch · Plastics · 80 × 60 × 50 mm

LEFT · **Iris Eichenberg** · *Knitted Hearts* · 1993–2007 · Brooch · Wool · Various sizes

OPPOSITE · **Otto Künzli** · *Heart* · 1985 · Brooch · Hard foam, lacquer, steel · 95 × 95 × 45 mm

SEE MORE of the **HEART FELT** cluster → 188

Are we secure in thinking contemporary jewellery speaks just with boundless expressions of love? Surely not, for a simple heart token will never fully conceal the complications that arise when you give something or when you're on the make. And, for the interested, there can be a real fascination in how something is made, or how many are produced. I am reminded of the Northern Soul subculture, in which rare, obscure records are acquired as signs of authenticity and status. Northern Soul records are reproduced but not mass-produced, and followers will pay substantial sums to own original labels.

Though it is rarely stated, contemporary jewellery has its own market economy that is driven by gift exchange and the recognition of artistry, craft values and signature in making sets belong within the field's giving circles. Works are made, sold, acquired, exchanged and passed on to celebrate life's *Crowning Moment*—those times when a milestone is reached, a goal achieved or a connection enriched. When a worn out work draws attention in an initiated crowd, it can resonate like the pause after a performance. The piece will evoke a maker's understanding about belonging, with status and authenticity invested in craft values and artistic conceptions about the roles jewellery plays. But these ideas are mere code to be scrambled when an audience teases apart the wearer's own intimated story employing the piece.

→ 190

Northern Soul devotees will sometimes engage in decoy practices, re-titling original labels in shops so as to make them invisible to the broader public. It's a street image that can be translated for thinking about art in industry. Within creative communities aligned with art markets, the commodity value of works is disguised. By an inverted economic law, value tends to flow from the intangible characteristics produced—the object as cultural and creative capital. The artist says something about the world and the place of his art within it.

Contemporary jewellers put forward propositions about jewellery. Often, they highlight jewellery's social role by drawing it out of its usual social contexts. Through radical expressions they might ask, Can jewellery be expressed through its relationship with clothing? Or is it possible to articulate jewellery's distinctions through performance or language, art or design?

OPPOSITE · **Benjamin Lignel** · *Manifest (I am)* · 2009 ·

Brooch/box · Screen-printed metal and stainless steel; fine gold and stainless steel · 41 × 33 mm

TOP · **Marc Monzó** · *Big Solitaire Brooch* · 2006 ·

Brooch · Silver, zirconia, steel · 65 × 80 mm

BOTTOM · **Roseanne Bartley** · *One on Every Corner* · 2006 ·

Brooch · Sterling silver, stainless steel, plastic · 12 × 65 × 65 mm

SEE MORE of the **CROWNING MOMENT** cluster → **190**

Artistry is always a negotiation about belonging. It unravels across communities in creative flashes. Perhaps for the most part this is because makers seek belonging through making. To spin this into gold all the roles in art are crucial—from the maker to the dealer to the collector. The makers need not be interested in their clientele to induce demand. Work is authentic because it has *genuine* meaning. The makers haven't even made it → 192 to sell. They have made it because they need to *Tell Tales*. The work will gain resonance if it mirrors how people think about being and belonging in the contemporary world. Resonance is an effect of the workmanship, the aesthetics or an association between ideas. Perhaps the makers have elaborated the social repertoire attached to a commonly used object, like jewellery.

The inspiration and impulses in art are usually viewed as separate to the controlled communication and cool design that companies use to differentiate their brands and offerings. An artist may highlight the commoditisation of culture through work, but this will still be elevated as comment. Increasingly, an idea of creativity attached to design is being distributed as the basis for commercial culture to manage personal distinctions.

Today, we are all designers. We assemble and share objects, sounds, images, links, likes, statuses and significant others to manage our distinctions. And the designers are the stars. They create the stories and archetypes that make it easy to know which brands are safe and which to stay away from. Individuality? Not so interested as long as I can move with relative ease across clubs, communities, networks and borders, picking up different forms of belonging along the way and developing artistry in appearing and disappearing. Brands try to cluster us as "young suburbans" or "money with brains". Better design approaches mean they can work in overdrive to keep up with our inventive sampling from the peripheries. Visibility means pulling off the rebel sell—achieving a swag story before swag goes out of fashion.

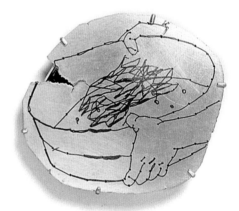

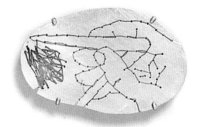

ABOVE · **Esther Knobel** · *The Mind in the Hand* · 2008 · Brooch · Silver, iron thread · 60 × 40 × 7 mm

OPPOSITE TOP · **Otto Künzli** · *The Manhattan Piece* · 1987 · Body piece · Rubber, brass, Uriol, steel, tin, book · 113 × 87 × 15 mm

OPPOSITE BOTTOM · **Herman Hermsen** · *The Nipple* · 2010 · Brooch · Photo, acrylic, pearls, silver · 70 × 40 mm

SEE MORE of the **TELL TALES** cluster → 192

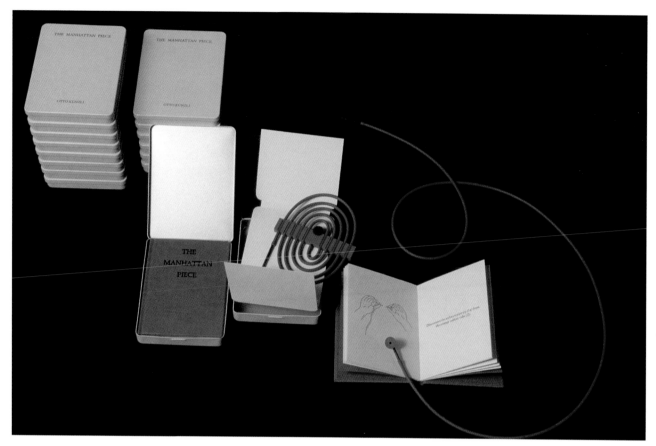

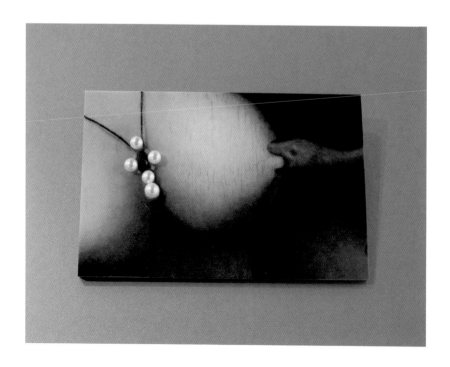

When our societies go hunting for cool, design plays the intermediary. Design drives mass culture, translating ideas about belonging into objects and signs that can be reproduced and distributed on a mass scale. In this way it allows ideas percolated in arts communities to trickle down into high-street retail. And because design is also beginning to drive the way we communicate through technologies, it facilitates a bubbling up of new belongings from our homes to culture at large.

Contemporary jewellery differentiates itself as a community by aligning with art and folding design approaches into making. It also emphasises authenticity in recognising craft ideals. For those interested, contemporary jewellery seems to offer something "real" amidst all the noise and traffic. It says Yes, I'm comfortable operating at *Face Value*. But I'd rather do it with a cheeky, animal grin.

→ 194

Design is evolving from an approach to a system that pervades every aspect of our lives. Whether it was ever intended or not, design is beginning to impose a kind of chaos theory onto our relations with the world. Expressions of belonging can become amplified building toward new trends and movements in culture. Commercial brands rely on this and will often promote aggressive forms of belonging. But by the same token, belonging can quickly turn political.

ABOVE · **Kiko Gianocca** · *Who Am I?* · 2008/11 · Rings · Gold, silver, polyurethane · Various sizes

OPPOSITE TOP · **Paul Derrez** · *Face Pendant* · 1994 · Pendant · Aluminium, resin · 50 × 60 × 20 mm

OPPOSITE BOTTOM · **Pavel Opocensky** · *Untitled* · 2008 · Brooch · Colorcore · 70 × 70 mm

SEE MORE of the **FACE VALUE** cluster → 194

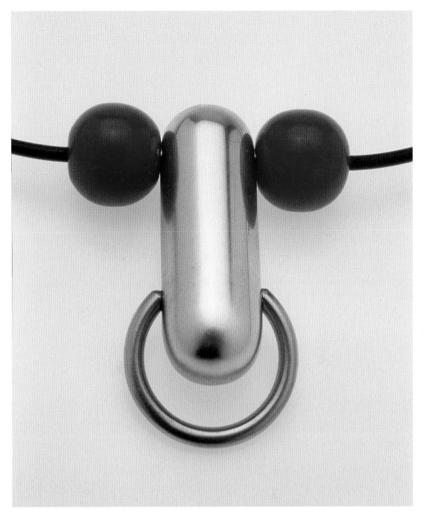

From the highways toward Tripoli to the main streets in Hackney, contemporary societies are undergoing profound political transformation. People are adopting certain objects and symbols, perhaps Adidas sportswear or an armband in revolutionary green, and wearing these out like jewellery to align themselves within societies where belonging has become the primary force for change. By manipulating the media, using social networks or even looting consumer goods, groups mirror the forms of belonging promoted by the established political order and the commercial forces laid out in its bed.

→ 196 Contemporary jewellery's *Modus Operandi* is embedded in how it positions itself as a community and the resonance of political work resides in the connection between the makers and the world on which they comment. Contemporary jewellery rarely enters into the political arena. But makers as artists do sample from the changing symbolic landscape for belonging, and the making experience can be shaped by a global awareness, even if the influence remains unconscious.

TOP · **Attai Chen** · *D_9* · 2010 · Brooch · Olive wood, silver, stainless steel · 80 × 50 × 5 mm
BOTTOM · **Benjamin Lignel** · *Manifest (Thank God)* · 2008 · Badge · Screen-printed acetate and paper, gold-plated steel · 56 × 56 mm
OPPOSITE · **Frédéric Braham** · *Putting on the Lotion* · 2007 · Neck piece · Body lotion, quartz pearl, plastic can, optical fibre, mica shimmer, industrial paint, magnets · 400 mm length
SEE MORE of the **MODUS OPERANDI** cluster → 196

TOP · **Bettina Speckner** · *Untitled (Brooch)* · 2006 · Brooch · Photo-etching in gold, zinc · 72 × 65 mm

BOTTOM · **Bas Bouman** · *Touch Wood* · 2007 · Neck piece · Oak, brass · 290 mm diameter

OPPOSITE · **Monika Brugger** · *Marianne en Roberts* · 2008 · Brooch · Silver, gold, stainless steel and fabric · 28 mm long

<u>SEE MORE</u> of the **NEVER FORGET** cluster → **198**

Perhaps it is best that contemporary jewellery does remain removed from the political. This is not to say that it could or should not make a political comment. Rather, the potential power of contemporary jewellery lies in the way it enriches connections, and it very rarely asks us to engage with serious intent.

Change often demands that you don't look back. Contemporary jewellery reminds us to *Never Forget*. → 198 And while it evokes symbols for our shared pasts, it also opens jewellery as a space for personal artistry, inviting you to establish your own links and memories using the object as token. In this sense, it offers us a form of belonging that is free.

That contemporary jewellery can accommodate such a range of identities and styles is reflective of its time. It has never been easier for makers to connect and to engage with others. Media resolves art with design, creating an energy that travels both ways. While design offers a common system for people around the world to connect, the potential in contemporary jewellery to express difference as belonging has been opened up through art influences.

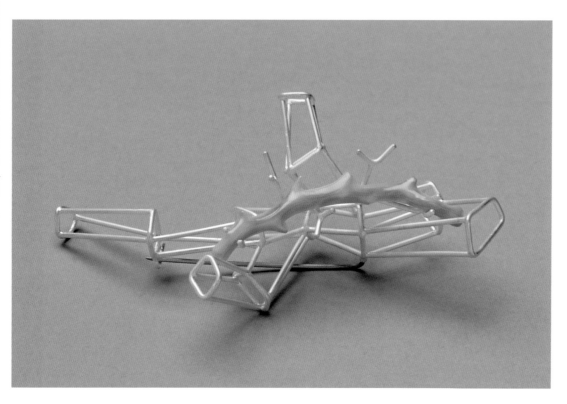

<u>TOP</u> · **Kimiaki Kageyama** · *Mountain Cherry Leaves* · 2010 · Brooch · Iron, natural akoya baroque pearl, gold, deep sea coral · 100 × 60 × 40 mm

<u>BOTTOM</u> · **Carlier Makigawa** · *Nature in Structure* · 2011 · Brooch · Sterling silver, coral · 100 × 40 × 50 mm

<u>OPPOSITE</u> · **Sam Tho Duong** · *Frozen* · 2011 · Neck piece · Silver, pearls, nylon · 60 × 150 × 560 mm

<u>SEE MORE</u> of the **EARTHLY DELIGHTS** cluster → **200**

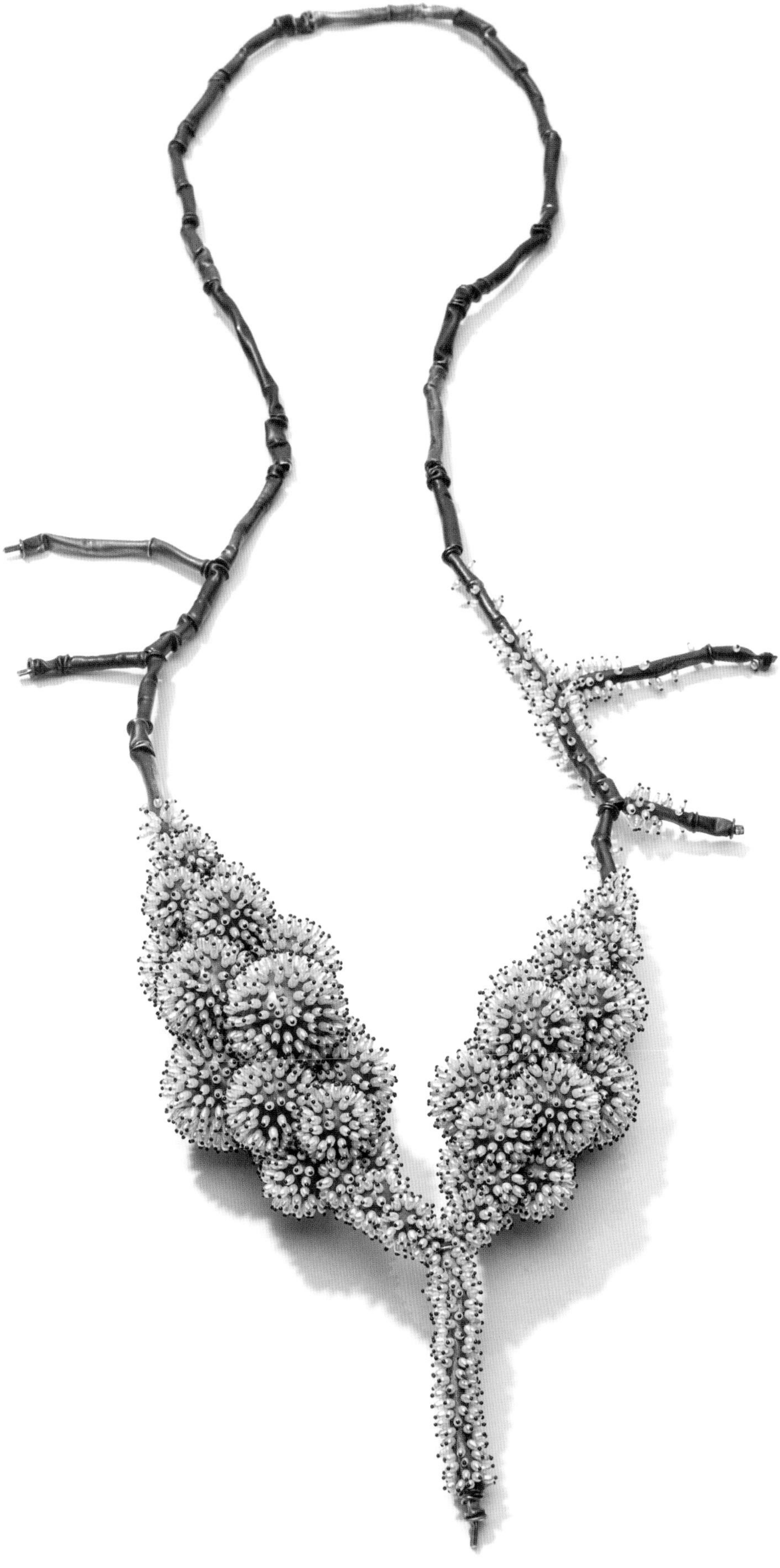

To understand how art and design might fit together, you can think about them as sets of objects that occupy a shared space. Together, they generate meaning through associations between ideas and forms, laying diverse types of thinking out in front of you. It's the same effect as might occur when you lay out all your personal belongings. These are discoveries placed before you, each with its own stories that now weave together as one. The points of connections are in the different ways in which something common is said.

Unexpected Pleasures works in the same way. It is the story of a group of makers who share diverse visions and ideas about the world that are common because they are focused through contemporary jewellery. They play on imagery that is foundational to our understanding of community and place. When

→ 200
→ 202

inventions upon our *Earthly Delights* and *Animal Instincts* are clustered alongside other contemporary works, they tell us to take care.

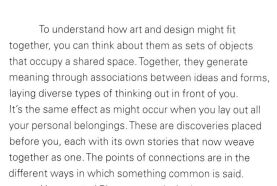

TOP · **Julia deVille** · *Trophy Mouse* · 2006 · Brooch · Mouse, jet, gold · 50 × 50 × 40 mm

BOTTOM · **Alexander Blank** · *Ed's Friend Duck* · 2009 · Brooch · Rigid foam, silver, Perspex, lacquer · 65 × 47 × 115 mm

OPPOSITE · **Felieke van der Leest** · *Yellow Kelly* · 2008 · Neck piece · Glass beads, textile, gold, plastic animal, cubic zirconia · 100 × 100 × 35 mm

SEE MORE of the **ANIMAL INSTINCTS** cluster → 202

A community maps itself out not only by the sense of commonality but also by connections shaped through history. Over time, different creative communities have sought to define their own histories in varying ways. For instance, in art, the relationship between artistic traditions and belonging across broader cultural stages has taken the artist's inspiration as central for finding new ways to express the nature of the times. Design has elaborated this concept. Invention marks the evolution of societies brought together by change in technologies. Communities have been integrated in to ever-expanding circles through a series of key *Turning Points*. These are moments where the cult status of a design object brings about a new sense of belonging tied to both personal transformation in the use experience and historical transformation that ripples out as consumers elaborate the symbolic value of design's changing language. Within this system, the idea of the turning point forms part of a mythology integral to commercial culture, through which design fulfills its stated role in society.

→ 204

OPPOSITE TOP · **Johanna Dahm** · *Stick* · 1982 · Pins · Anodised aluminium · 150 × 1.8 mm

OPPOSITE BOTTOM · **Warwick Freeman** · *Large Star* · 1990 · Brooch · Pearl shell, lacquer · 60 × 60 mm

ABOVE · **Esther Knobel** · *Warrior Brooches* · 1983–5 · Brooch · Recycled painted tin can, stainless steel wire, elastic thread · 150 × 120 mm

SEE MORE of the **TURNING POINTS** cluster → **204**

It would be misleading to believe that contemporary jewellery's turning points are simply defined by those moments when the field has established links with expressions within art and inventions in design. Some of the most understated expressions in contemporary jewellery are recognised in hindsight as its key moments because they distill thinking that has come to inform how the field thinks about what it does. And because many of the seminal works in contemporary jewellery have an everyday quality, able to be worn out and shown off, their recognition relates also to the way they have stimulated exchange.

Jewellery is present across our many lives. It marks the predictable events and unexpected pleasures in the real world. Contemporary jewellery too has an everyday poetry, amplified by the _Held Secrets_ of the maker. So it speaks for belonging in many unique ways. Because many of the seminal works in contemporary jewellery have this everyday quality— they are designed to be worn out and shown off—their historical importance abides by a logic distinct to those in operation in art and design cultures. Their recognition relates primarily to the ways they have stimulated exchange between makers, wearers and those engaged with contemporary jewellery. That is to say, while contemporary jewellery has mirrored forms of belonging on the "outside", the community's vision of itself and the world at large is mediated through jewellery values and a love of making.

→ 206

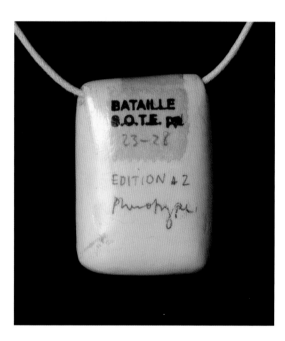

<u>ABOVE</u> · **James McAllister** · _Contained Erotic Text_ · 2009 · Pendant · Paper, cotton cloth/thread, plaster, ink, varnish · 55 × 40 × 14 mm

<u>RIGHT</u> · **Margaret West** · _Shadow of Faded Daffodil_ · 2007 · Brooch · Basalt, paint, silver · 90 × 85 × 5 mm

<u>OPPOSITE</u> · **Leonor Hipólito** · _Object for Dreams_ · 2006 · Neck piece · Resin, silver, silk · Dimensions variable

<u>SEE MORE</u> of the **HELD SECRETS** cluster → **206**

CHAPTER THREE
Reflections

In any broad-ranging conversation there are always many different voices, which help reflect on the nature of the subject. The three following essays— two current and one from fifteen years ago— offer different perspectives on how contemporary jewellery engages with ideas and how it might further evolve as a creative expression.

→ 96 Glenn Adamson proffers his concern that whilst metal has always been a jeweller's best friend, contemporary jewellery has generally failed to consider the dark side of metal as an enemy to the body, and in doing so has failed to challenge us in the way that the broader art field has done. He suggests jewellery is commonly used as gentle reassurance, not as an expression of more difficult painful emotions. Yet Glenn sees signs of a broader exploration of human emotions in recent contemporary jewellery, implying jewellery might eventually live up to its full potential.

Glenn Adamson is a theorist, writer, researcher and educator with a keen interest in craft. He is author of *Thinking Through Craft*, co-editor of *Journal of Modern Craft* and editor of *The Craft Reader.* He is deputy head of research and head of graduate studies at the Victoria and Albert Museum in London, where his most recent project was an exhibition called Postmodernism: Style and Subversion 1970–1990 held in late 2011.

→ 102 Liesbeth den Besten addresses the issue of beauty in contemporary jewellery. She reflects that beauty has no "general recipe", and that it will be either ignored or attacked depending on how aesthetics are being challenged in art or design. Using the exhibition programme of Galerie Ra in Amsterdam, Liesbeth shows how contemporary jewellery experimented with common ideals of beauty, adapting its opposite values— imperfect, unfinished, exaggerated, formless and so on—as a new "no taste" aesthetic as a way to challenge classical ideas of beauty in jewellery. However, whilst beauty may be rejected intellectually, it has always been the inspiration for jewellery, and in turn jewellery is the quintessential celebration of beauty.

Liesbeth den Besten is an art historian working within the field of contemporary jewellery as a writer, lecturer and exhibition curator. She is author of *On Jewellery*, a comprehensive overview of contemporary jewellery art from the late 1960's to today, and she was guest curator for an exhibition called Unleashed! An Overview of Rule-Breaking Jewellery held at the Museum voor Moderne Kunst in Arnhem in 2011–2012.

Peter Dormer's critical views are as relevant → 108 today as when they were written fifteen years ago. The abstract of this essay centres on the relationship between jewellery and the body, with attention to how it is portrayed in the photograph. Dormer argues that contemporary jewellery has used the body to reclaim jewellery as art, abstracting its form as a canvas for ideas. He suggests the powerful influence of photography on contemporary jewellery lies in the jewellers' desire to use the photograph as background material to frame their ideas and personality. Emphasising that "wearability" is a design problem, Dormer discusses the physical and emotional values of wearing jewellery and questions the validity of some suggestions by contemporary jewellers—via the photograph—that their unconventional objects are easily worn.

Peter Dormer (1949–1996) was a highly respected writer on craft, design, and contemporary jewellery. His books include *The New Jewellery* (with Ralph Turner), *Meanings of Modern Design, Design Since 1945, The Art of the Maker* and *Jewellery of Our Time: Art, Ornament and Obsession* (with Helen W. Drutt English).

Metal Against the Body

By Glenn Adamson

A set of imperfect teeth, fiercely gritted, surrounded by two frames: first, a pair of lips, flared wide open; and inside them, a hard layer of gold encasing the gums.

Saliva pools inside the lower lip, testament to the discomfort of holding the pose. This ferocious image is part of an installation of objects, film and photographs entitled *Hard Wear* by the American artist Lauren Kalman. It's not exactly what we have come to expect from contemporary jewellery. That tradition (for despite the word *contemporary*, it is now a tradition, going back fifty years) is rarely so vivid in its encounter with the human form. This genre revolves around the body, yes, but much as moons revolve around a distant planet. The great craft critic Rose Slivka, in a 1983 article, put it like this:

> "It is in orbit around the body, a galaxy of planets whirling on their dervishes. Jewellery is now a body cage and a mind expander."[1]

Improbable shapes of all persuasions have been fitted over the neck and wrist, pierced through clothing, and even projected in light against the human form. But what about the "wearers" of these objects, if we can call them that? They might as well be thousands of miles away. If you look at any book of contemporary jewellery, you'll see three types of images: the ornament isolated in the frame, probably against a white seamless backdrop; a tight crop, in which the ornament sits against an isolated body part, a forearm or shoulder; or a portrait-style image, in which the model assumes a posture of impassive assurance. No matter how extreme the body cage or mind expander, or how much outré panache it might bring someone in day-to-day life— Marjorie Schick's vast rainbow-coloured ruff, or Caroline Broadhead's translucent plastic cylinder encasing

→ 98
→ 65

a woman's head—in photos, it's as if everything is perfectly normal.

Those images are telling us something: despite its apparent unconventionality, contemporary jewellery has a fairly conservative heart. This is surprising, given that some of the field's leading lights have drawn directly from the deep well of constructivism, the avant-garde movement which sought to radicalise European society through a complete rethinking of everyday things. A strong stylistic current flows forward from that origin, from Margaret De Patta in 1950s America (she got constructivism from the source, having studied with László Moholy-Nagy), through Gijs Bakker and Emmy van Leersum in the Netherlands in the 1960s, to Susanna Heron in the 1980s, here in the UK. All of these artists adopted constructivism's abstraction and dynamism. But don't go looking to any of them for social revolution; they were formalists, pure and simple. The reception of their work tends to presume a vague "challenge" to accepted notions of wearability and luxury. But it is unlikely that this avant-garde impulse was ever deeply felt, at least in a political sense. There are occasional exceptions to the rule—the post-punk antagonist Bernhard Schobinger springs to mind—but even so, I've yet to meet a contemporary jeweller who is motivated by a visceral hatred of Cartier.

Rather, the field has adopted an approach that we might call "alternative commercialism." It is a stance more like that of the surrealists, the constructivists' more permissive cousins, rather than the constructivists themselves. Salvador Dalí, Meret Oppenheim and Man Ray embraced the ridiculous and the repulsive, maintaining a highbrow tone all the while.

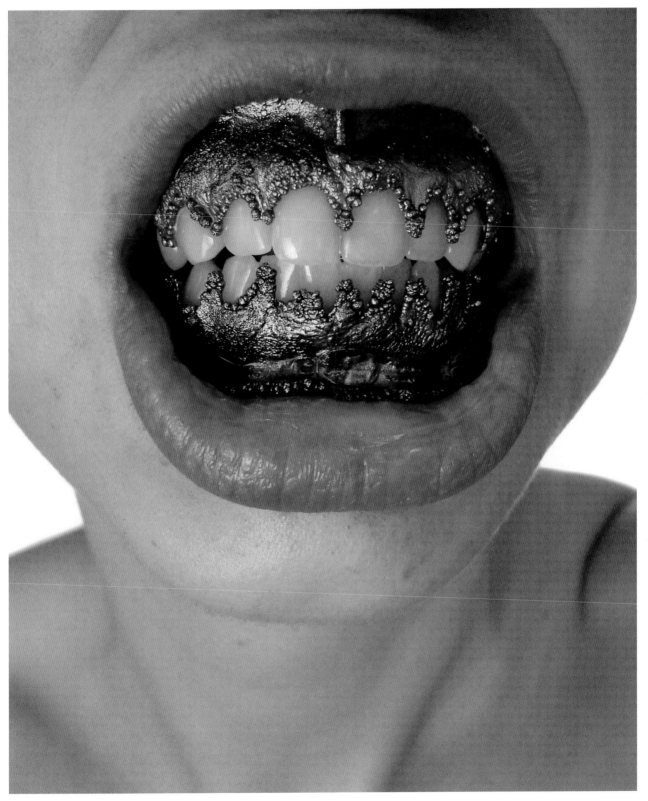

ABOVE · **Lauren Kalman** · *Hard Wear (Oral Rims)* · 2006 · Mouthpiece · Inkjet print, laminated on acrylic, gold-plated electroformed copper · 584 × 762 mm

PAGE 99 · **Marjorie Schick** · *Spiraling Over the Line* · 2008 · Painted canvas, wood and brass rivets · 1,700 × 914 × 914 mm when worn

PAGE 101 · **Wilfredo Prieto** · *One* · 2008 · Thousands of fake diamonds, one real diamond · Dimensions variable

The combination was brilliant marketing, especially in Dalí's case, and it may not be a coincidence that one of the Spanish maestro's favoured media was jewellery. In the late 1940s he recycled some of his greatest hits— Mae West's lips, a leering eye, a metamorphosing hand—into the form of precious stones. A promotional shot of the collection denotes strangeness without actually being disturbing. The model stares goggle-eyed into space, textbook surrealist style. But you know she'll set down these pretty baubles the moment the shutter closes and probably think nothing of it. As superficially bizarre as they might be, Dalí's jewels are not literally *against* the body, even though one is held in the mouth (in the manner of Kalman's gold-carapaced gums); they are only *near* it.

How could we hope to match the great machines and speeding locomotives of the Industrial Revolution?

This seems a failure of imagination, for of all materials known to us, metal is easily the most threatening. Pick your cliché: a knife at the throat; a gun at the temple; a safe falling from a height. Or just pop some tin-foil in your mouth. Metal hurts. Even when it is made to serve our interests, it tends to remind us of our own limitations. Trapped in our soft, slow, weak bodies, how could we hope to match the great machines and speeding locomotives of the Industrial Revolution or the monstrous capacity of science-fiction cyborgs? Think of Charlie Chaplin caught in a giant set of gears or Andy Warhol's multiplied car crashes (or for that matter, the same motif in the work of contemporary sculptors as diverse as John Chamberlain, Cai Guo-Qiang, Jeremy Deller and Charles Ray). As these artists seem to have noticed, metal, the jeweller's best friend, has historically been a great enemy of the human body.

Don't get me wrong: metal can be lovely and useful. (I'm eating with a fork as I write this.) But it is striking how little contemporary jewellery has attended to the less friendly implications of its favourite material. This strikes me as an opportunity missed. Of course, jewellery can be made of just about any material (though it's interesting that plastic, which shares many of metal's unsettling physical and social qualities, is another common choice, and is just as rarely presented as alien to the human frame). But all jewellery stands, at least potentially, against the body and not just alongside

it. Of all artistic media, it is the one best positioned (literally) to cover the full range of human affect, not only having and holding, but also hatred and horror. Why have so few chosen to explore this dark potential of body ornament? One reason, perhaps, is so many people believe that, as the critic Peter Dormer once put it,

"the potency [of craft] can be summarised in one word: *consolation*." [2]

Even when people look to the extreme edges of a practice like jewellery making, they seem to want reassurance—certainly not a genuine assault, and at most a gentle demand that is easily met. This instinct is not necessarily to be disdained. It is part of the humanism that has always infused modern craft. If industry and technology, those supremely metallic fields of endeavour, are quite literally superhuman, then artisanal making seems to uphold the smaller-scale values of the personal, the affective, even the familial. In the public imagination, craft is thought of as being passed down through the generations, from mothers and fathers to sons and daughters. Even the size and structure of a typical artisan workshop is reminiscent of a household. These are means by which craft lays claim to the precious value of intimacy. But as we all know, families can be dysfunctional. And intimacy, too, can hurt.

Consider *Untitled (Portrait of Ross in L.A.)*, 1991, by Felix Gonzales-Torres—an early example of "relational aesthetics" (that is, the inclusion of the audience in the form of the work). The physical makeup of the sculpture is simple enough: a pile of store-bought sweets, each in a brightly coloured wrapper. Each viewer is invited to take and eat a single candy. It is a tactic used extensively in Gonzales-Torres' work—he has also given away printed pieces of paper and other materials— but in the case of *Portrait of Ross in L.A.*, the work is freighted with an unusual emotional burden. Ross was the artist's lover and was at the time dying of AIDS in Los Angeles. The sculpture functions as a living "portrait," in the sense that it is initially installed at Ross's healthy body weight. As visitors remove each candy, they inexorably reduce the pile, mimetically reprising the wasting away of his body, the pain that love can bring. (The fact that Gonzales-Torres himself died of AIDS in 1996 makes the work even more poignant.) There is of course nothing handmade about the sculpture—it consists entirely of found objects—yet in its attention to detail, colour and the artist's incorporation of many hands (which place and then remove the candies), it has all the humanism, and some of the material nuance, that we often associate with craft.

This idea of art as a relational project, with all the possibility for emotional intensity that the concept of family entails, has recently been brought to the world of jewellery by the London-based artist Maisie Broadhead. → 139 Her photographs are closely based on historic paintings but star her own family members and intimate friends, many of whom are prominent craft artists in their own right (Caroline Broadhead, mentioned previously, is her mother). Each of her vignettes features a ring, brooch or necklace of her own design. Far from sporting these ornaments impassively, though, her subjects organise themselves into exquisite fictions around them. The astronomical structure that Slivka described is thereby reversed—here it is the bodies that orbit the ornaments, not the other way round.

their peers are not working against the body in any explicit way, but there is still an element of antagonism in their work, a desire to unsettle

Kalman's and Broadhead's photographs might be taken as apt bookends for the *Unexpected Pleasures* project, for it operates in the richly textured terrain marked out by these two young artists—between the aggressive and the affective. At times the exhibition comes on pretty gently, but it also includes sections like → 116 *Worn Out*, a sign that the psychic space being described is a little bit bigger than we might have thought. And then we circle back to the title, with its insistence on surprise, and then back through the works, which prove to be as unexpected as advertised. There are several works of a disturbing nature: Tiffany Parbs' blister → 148 → 126 jewellery, Lisa Walker's necklace of disembodied doll → 55 parts, Karl Fritsch's rusty *Screw Ring*—and beyond these images of outright violence, many poetic evocations of uncertainty and melancholy.

→ 198 Kiko Gianocca's *Never Been There* brooches, for example, mute black rectangles which look like miniature On Kawara paintings awaiting their dates, prove to be anti-maps of the memory: their reverse sides show various unvisited tourist destinations. In *Unexpected Pleasures,* this stark cancellation of jewellery's most familiar functions (in this case, to act as a souvenir) is typical. There is, of course, great individuality of vision, but one artist after another operates by directly contradicting our expectations about what jewellery should do. Rather than proffering

exciting new objects to incite our desire, as Dalí did, these artists tend to dangle the prospect of easy pleasure in front of us only to withdraw it. Thus, Otto Künzli's big red heart, a symbol of affection → 75 wrought in impassive plastic, sits against the wearer's chest like a dead weight. Künzli both acknowledges our need to materialize emotion in the physical form of jewellery—our desire, as it were, to wear our heart on our sleeve—and suggests through broad caricature that no object could ever perform that role adequately.

Something similar can be said for Ben Lignel, a Parisian jeweller and theorist who focuses on another part of the body—the ear. In the series *Thinking of You*, → 198 he has created a series of commissioned brooches in which the physical features of a loved one's ear (that of a partner, friend or child) reproduced in painted silver. Though this project is technically similar to Kalman's *Oral Rims*, in that Lignel is limning an unusually sensitive body part, he does not find it necessary to literally apply it to the skin to achieve an unsettling effect. Instead he uses the gambit of the eerily accurate copy, one of the ways that craft can most readily echo (and hence comment on) the world beyond itself. He has written of Victorian mourning lockets, which often included the hair of a deceased relative, as an important precursor for these works. Like the lockets, his brooches mark emotional attachment through the uncanny indexical trace of the body, so that they are (in his words) "poised between remains and representation."[3] Lignel's jewellery suggests that the double-sided quality of metal, both intimacy and discomfort, can operate at a distance. He, Künzli, Gianocca and their peers are not working against the body in any explicit way, but there is still an element of antagonism in their work, a desire to unsettle. Rather than adopting contemporary jewellery's customary position, in close proximity to the human frame but not really invading its physical and psychological space, the artists in this show want to cut right in. They do offer unexpected pleasures, but only by persuading us to realign our ideas about pleasure itself.

I have emphasised the degree to which contemporary jewellery has begun to explore the full breadth of human emotion, including the registers of sorrow, pain and rage that the field previously tended to ignore. But this is only a small part of a much broader transformation in the arts, in which the value of discipline—both in the sense of conceptual rigor and in the policing of boundaries between formerly discrete fields such as art, craft and design—has yielded to a more humanist, affective set of priorities. This shift has allowed makers of all kinds to drop the somewhat strained posture of detached conceptualism as it was practiced in the late twentieth-century. In this way,

a long-anticipated fluidity across disciplines has finally arrived, with emotion as its binder. Gabriel Craig's aperçu regarding Lauren Kalman is apposite here:

"she is the child of Art and Craft's divorce; quite indifferent to their past quarrels, she loves them both. After all, they are her parents."[4]

So too is Lignel's observation that

"the fact that contemporary jewellery, in most cases, "could be used" goes a long way towards establishing its hybrid allegiance (to the functional and the non-functional at the same time)."[5]

Of course, craftspeople have been claiming for decades that they were dismantling the boundaries between their own concerns and those of fine artists and designers. But this doesn't mean much unless the traffic is two-way, as well as both-and. It is not enough for jewellers to ape constructivists and surrealists; there must be genuine interchange among practitioners working in different ways.

In *Unexpected Pleasures*, we do indeed see the signs of this fluidity. In its unabashed humanism, both ugly and reassuring, the exhibition takes a rightful place in a visual landscape that extends far outside the realm of jewellery. That landscape is populated by works like Wilfredo Prieto's *One*, a floor-based sculpture somewhat reminiscent of Gonzales-Torres's pile of candy, whose materials are officially listed as "thousands of fake diamonds, one real diamond". It also includes Roni Horn's *Gold Mats for Ross and Felix*—simply two sheets of gold leaf, one laying atop another—a sculpture whose gut-wrenching emotional impact is derived from the elegant concision in which the two dead lovers have been portrayed. You might think we have travelled a long way here away from craft, into the remote realms of abstraction and Duchamp-style appropriation. Yet the emotional registers that these sculptures plumb so effectively—frustration, humour, elegy, and sorrow—would be impossible to achieve without deep consideration of the issues that have always animated jewellery: the way that humans bring value to things like precious stones and metal, clutching them close. In the light that glints from Prieto's 99.999-percent-fake heap or the delicately rumpled negative space sandwiched between Horn's two sheaves of gold, we catch a fleeting glimpse of a widely shared ambition: to live up to the possibilities that jewellery has always afforded.

This essay is based on a lecture originally delivered to the Society of North American Goldsmiths (SNAG) in Seattle, in June 2011.

The Trouble with Beauty

By Liesbeth den Besten

Galerie Ra, established in 1976, is one of the most influential jewellery galleries in the world and one of the first to explore new definitions of contemporary jewellery thanks to the openness to new ideas of its director, Paul Derrez.

When Derrez started his gallery, he was interested in the industrial and formalist approach of the Dutch—and in a certain way also European—jewellery scene at that time. But the gallery went on to introduce more colourful British jewellery, textile trends and the painterly and expressive gold jewellery of Robert Smit.

After thirty-five years this privately run gallery in the heart of Amsterdam is still exploring new developments in international jewellery.

One of the biggest mistakes you could make as a first-year art-history undergraduate in the 1970s was to find something "beautiful". Students had to unlearn the word instantly. "Beauty" was not considered "objective". *Beautiful* was a term excluded from intellectual discourse.

In the art of that time, "beauty" was an intellectually charged concept. Barnett Newman, the preeminent exponent of American colour-field painting wrote in 1948: "The impulse of modern art is the desire to destroy beauty". It was an extreme statement, provocatively illustrating his position. According to Newman, the driving force of modernism was to replace beauty with the sublime. An artwork should not illustrate, represent or symbolise anything other than its autonomous self.

In the late 1960s, jewellery design was also in the grip of modernism. It led to emotionally detached jewellery objects—large, stark, gleaming and imposing. More demonstrative than decorative. "The ornament is for me a thing in itself. It is an object", wrote the jewellery designer Françoise van den Bosch in 1974, succinctly expressing the direction that Dutch jewellery design was taking at the time

Galerie Ra was founded in 1976, at the height of modernism, as a venue in which experimental jewellery could be shown. Ten years later, there was little trace in a literal sense of modernism in jewellery. But it did appear to have left a legacy: a concentration of geometric forms and a taboo on traditional materials that were perceived as being too "seductive"

The innate beauty of gold, silver and precious stones was observed as something suspect. It was a quality that was regarded as distracting from form. Gijs Bakker suggested in a famous dialogue with fellow designer Robert Smit in 1986, "Another merit, and a very important one—is that sentimental artisanship has disappeared from the practice of making jewellery, and the flirtation with expensive materials has become pointless".

OPPOSITE · *Paul Derrez* · 2010 · Director of Galerie Ra

TOP · *Galerie Ra* · 2011 · Nes 120, exterior

BOTTOM · *Galerie Ra* · 2011 · Nes 120, interior

GALERIE RA

foto: Rogers/Versluys

LAM DE WOLF 9 NOVEMBER T/M 7 DECEMBER 1985
VIJZELSTRAAT 80, 1017 HL AMSTERDAM

However, what is "sentimental" to Bakker is essential to Smit. The latter was interested in self-expression, and he needed both artisanship and a personal signature to achieve it. After a gap of more than a decade, Smit had resumed jewellery making, which he exhibited at the Galerie Ra. Smit excoriated modernism: "This so-called jewellery, the fruits of a collectively shared lack of imagination, is without meaning, little more than the pretentious equivalent of commonplace bells and whistles, the kind of which it so ostentatiously rebels against." Bakker and Smit identified two contrived extremes: conceptualism, and formalism versus expressionism. From then on, anything was possible between these two extremes.

Looking back at what was to come over the following decade, I ask myself what were the consequences for modernism of experiencing beauty in jewellery. The struggle for new ideals was coupled at least in the jewellery world with taking swipes at anything that did not conform to one's own view. While the classic idea of beauty in jewellery was being questioned, the gleam of gold and precious stones was replaced by the gleam of the autonomous form produced in industrial materials.

Modernism led to a new aesthetic. The 1970s were characterised by what might be called the "futurism" of stark, stripped and exaggerated jewellery. But even "futurism" can be superseded. Out of modernism another experimental direction evolved with a different aesthetic. How did jewellery makers resolve this challenge after a period of aesthetic deconstruction? Where did the beauty lie in their jewellery? When neither traditional craftsmanship nor the abstraction of the pure geometric form of modernism could define the beauty of jewellery, what was then the new ideal of beauty?

The concept of beauty merits further examination. For centuries it has been the subject of debate. Without attempting a brief history of aesthetics, I would suggest a few issues that are relevant in the context of jewellery. Beauty is not only linked to concepts such as exquisite, radiant, gleaming or pure, but also to such terms as *harmony*, *balance*, *order* and *symmetry*. At one time art and beauty were synonymous, but the modern world has severed this connection. Beauty for those who choose to see it can be found in decay and chaos. Our feeling for beauty is culturally determined and continually subject to change.

In 1986 Paul Derrez, Galerie Ra's founder, suggested "the concept of jewellery is now much more broadly interpreted, and the phase of "positive discrimination", which the profession needed in order to strengthen its identity, has moved onto a general

interest in design, in which wearability and functionality play less of a role. Alongside jewellery, Galerie Ra also shows objects, small consumer products and so on".

Galerie Ra regularly showed Gijs Bakker, Beppe Kessler, Herman Hermsen, Marion Herbst, Otto Künzli, Lam de Wolf, Daniel Kruger, Esther Knobel and Petra Hartman. The idea of "anything goes" appears something to be celebrated at this time. Lam de Wolf and Marjorie Schick made large wearable objects from painted wooden sticks or papier mâché. Kai Chan and Julia Manheim made sculptural crossover works and even jewellery that deliberately sets out to offend us, such as, Petra Hartman's *The Dirty Woman* was exhibited in the gallery.

In the violent eruptions of colour, form and decoration, or in the exaggerated expressions of kitsch, there are parallels to be drawn with Italian postmodernists from the Memphis and Studio Alchimia movements. Galerie Ra also organised exhibitions of vases, hats, shoes and domestic objects, as well as autonomous objects rooted in the British craft tradition.

In the 1990s Galerie Ra's focus changed to wearable jewellery, by Annelies Planteijdt, Warwick Freeman, Esther Knobel, Birgit Laken, Georg Dobler, Carlier Makigawa, Peter Mellema, Stephan Seyffert and Karl Fritsch, among others.

In this period many jewellery designs were still made based on geometric methodology. In the strict word it was no longer modernism, but basic geometric principles still seemed to provide a safe refuge.

A notable feature of Galerie Ra were the photographs Paul Derrez commissioned for every gallery bulletin to illustrate the work that he exhibited from Anna Beeke to Theo Baart. They share a curious ambiguity; beautiful-looking young men and women show jewellery or objects that have nothing to do with conventional ideas of beauty. In one notable example, taken for Georg Dobler's exhibition, the model stares, almost as if in amazement at her arm, around which a rectangular, three-dimensional metal bracelet has been pushed. The viewer's gaze is drawn to a thin fluttering handkerchief in her hand as if the photographer is trying

to soften the tough-looking construction on her arm. This bracelet has nothing to do with seductive beauty, and Anna Beeke was very much aware of it in her photography. Thus the model in her photographs often has the supplementary function of an intermediary.

Gijs Bakker always had a preference for beautiful models to show his designs. "That is staged, that is plastic, that is effective, that is theatre". He has also said: "I search for an abstraction that recognises all heads and all bodies—an impersonal body that doesn't distract from what it's about". At that point the human body was already so dominant in his jewellery that a beautiful model would have been a distraction. His jewellery from 1991 may be interpreted from the viewpoint of existing ideals of beauty. Bakker communicated this in Ra's bulletin. It included a large photograph of his Waterman brooch— a black-and-white image of a male nude, kneeling and caught in the act of pouring a bucket of water over his back. But instead of water, a cascade of tiny diamonds spills out over the brooch—the ultimate seductive beauty. On the other side is a photographic triptych. Each section portrays an older woman, wearing a different necklace in which physical and geometric elements attempt to find equilibrium.

The necklaces are made from flat gold bars that frame an ornament, the first a close-up photograph of a perfectly toned male torso, the second a hand and the third a piece of meat (entitled Roastbeef). The female model wearing the necklaces has a face that bears the traces of age and is lined by life. The images are set against a series of suggestive words: skin, vain, diamond, meat, pearl, body, gleam, mortal, muscle, wet, drop, nipple, fold". In text and image, Bakker touches on the enigma of beauty. While some critics, myself included, have interpreted these jewellery designs as a comment on the classical ideal of beauty, I also see them now as revealing a certain humanity, call it sentimentality, from which, in theory, Bakker has always distanced himself. They are designs that are enhanced and strengthened by the model wearing them. Bakker has always had an aversion toward the subordinate, ornamental function of jewellery, but in this case he was able to unite object and subject, with our ideals on beauty as the intermediary.

Like Bakker, Otto Künzli rejects the traditional ornamental role of jewellery. His Fragments collection drew many kinds and concepts of beauty together. It comprised a series of fragments of traditional ornate picture frames, some gilded with gold leaf, on fine steel cable, as a reference to the way in which pictures hang in galleries and museums. The picture frame wraps around the wearer's face. In Künzli's words, "A necklace and picture frame are edification, veneration, distinction, embellishment, homage, crowning, perfection". By restricting himself to fragments rather than using the complete frame, he is suggesting the imperfection of the wearer. According to Künzli, ornament is "an expression of the awareness of imperfection, of that outside paradise". By making use of imperfection, Künzli appears to be consciously connecting to a contemporary concept of beauty, which is neither harmonious nor elevated, but may be unpleasant and painful.

Marion Herbst (1944–1995) always liked to target sacred cows, and it is interesting to see her approach to addressing the notion of beauty. Her exhibition at Galerie Ra titled Irresponsible Design consisted of a collection of colourfully painted straw-and-papier-mâché boxes, some of which came with unidentifiable appendages that deliberately set out to be transgressive. The work was conspicuously hand crafted and made a point of rejecting skill. While the boxes did have hinges and could be closed, they had little to do with functional design. Herbst clearly set out deliberately to subvert conventional preconceptions about objects. She used vernacular processes, domestic materials and forms that had nothing to do with perfection. While the results appear to be light, innocent and mischievous, their result, as she intended, was to provoke and irritate many of her contemporaries. From the aesthetic perspective of the time, they were indeed "irresponsible".

Adri Hattink (1949–1998) also used an exhibition at Galerie Ra to attack conventional ideas of perfection, with a collection that set out to banish every connotation of the traditional qualities of gold- and silversmithing. He forged iron and copper with a direct bluntness, and yet, despite all his efforts to achieve exactly the opposite, the very imperfection of the results gave these objects an immense appeal and beauty. It was an approach that became widespread at the end of the 1980s among the gold- and silversmiths trained at the Rietveld Academy in Amsterdam by Onno Boekhoudt. And in the course of the decade, the idea of finding aesthetic quality—beauty—in imperfection rather than perfection gradually replaced the aesthetic of modernism.

Beauty is not often a subject of discussion in the design world. So it is interesting to find Bakker and van Leersum producing what amounts to a manifesto in 1967 that uses the term *aesthetic unity*. It is an issue that designers have managed to skirt around, but it is impossible to avoid. Jewellery, which is the quintessential celebration of beauty, cannot do without it. Beauty has always been the inspiration of the jeweller. Yet the concept of beauty is problematic. It suffers from negative connotations, such as "empty aestheticism". Anything that shimmers and shines is often associated with having no content. The Norwegian art historian Jorunn Veiteberg once suggested that

"The use of shiny fabrics such as velvet and silk, brilliant gemstones, silver and gold, is difficult to see as anything other than an urge to create something that is beautiful, and so to pay homage to beauty as a value. But perhaps this is also one of the reasons why today's textile and jewellery artists rarely use such materials?"

And if they do use them, it is done with an almost malicious undertone, like Stephan Seyffert's collection of shiny silver rings mounted with gemstones (exhibited at Galerie Ra in 1992–93).

There is no general recipe for beauty. Every period has its own ideals. The incompleteness, imperfection, lack of polish, formlessness and shrieking palette of the late 1980s and 1990s were all appropriated by the experimentalists who showed their work at Galerie Ra. There were also other appropriations: the use of exaggeration, scale shift and irony. All of them were deployed as strategies to avoid the trap of the classic idea of beauty as being about harmony, a concept that was too closely connected to the old-fashioned view of gold- and silversmithing as a craft and also to the modernism of the 1970s.

Nevertheless, the pursuit of the ideal of beauty is not easily denied. Galerie Ra's exhibition programme from the 1990s onward testifies to this. Even Paul Derrez could not resist or ignore the attraction and beauty of gems and colours in the work of contemporaries such as Daniel Kruger. In the 1990s beauty was once again discovered.

This text is a slightly revised version of an essay originally published to mark Galerie Ra's thirtieth anniversary as part of the Radiant 30 Years Ra *catalogue. Three essays covered three decades. The essay "1986–1996: Contemporary Jewellery and the Problem of Beauty", dealing with the period from 1986 to 1996, was one of three that each dealt with a different decade.*

The Body and Jewellery

By Peter Dormer

One of the most striking and minimalist images in the last thirty years of art jewellery was created by Gijs Bakker—it is a mark left by a wire band pulled tight around an upper arm. The band is taken off; the imprint in the flesh remains.

→ 63

It is a clever image—conceptual and fetishistic. It is a fine demonstration of that commonplace of contemporary art-production artspeak—"mark making". Of course without the photograph, this particular piece of mark making would have been lost to us. Photography wields an immensely powerful influence over artists and especially those who work in jewellery, because it is the way in which their work is communicated to the world and to posterity in an ideal position, on an ideal body.

Some artists and designers, notably Gijs Bakker, have produced work which uses the photograph as an integral part of the jewellery. Sometimes this jewellery is easily wearable, sometimes it is wearable only in the sense that it is best seen worn in a photograph. A good example is provided by Gijs Bakker's flower pieces such as *Dew Drop*, in which a huge photograph of a rose (with a dewdrop) is laminated between plastic and worn as a neck piece. Although this is a real object

and Bakker has produced many such real objects, it is for most of us a "virtual" object, a theoretical object in that it works ideally as a photograph in a book or in a magazine. For most people it is not a functional piece of jewellery and many more people will enjoy it vicariously than would wear it for themselves.

Another well-known piece of Bakker is *The Tongue*. In many cultures (such as that of the Maori) the protruding tongue is a gesture of power, and in this brooch the balancing of a cut diamond on the tongue gives that gesture some style and irony. It is a gift for a deconstructionist literary critic. In Western culture, the tongue is used to poke fun at something, and Bakker is well known for trying to prick what he regards as the pretensions of "precious" jewellery.

In his book *The Body* a collection of photographic images of the human body, ranging from medico-scientific imagery via sideshow freaks to erotica—William A. Ewing writes:

"Darker themes characterise much late twentieth-century photography of the naked figure. This is partly in reaction to what are perceived as particularly troubled times for the body, and partly because nudity has become such a commonplace motif in advertising that serious photographers believe that some shock therapy is needed in order to reclaim the body for art."

This comment, especially the notion of reclaiming the body for art, is interesting from the art-jewellery perspective, for it might be argued that jewellers have

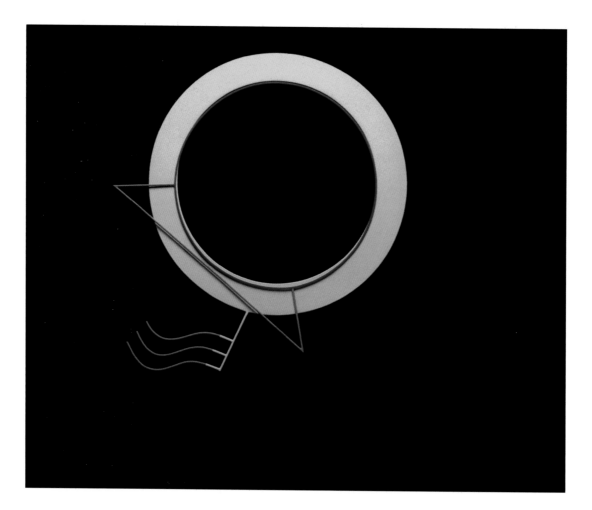

used the body to reclaim jewellery as art. That is to say, not content with using the humdrum idea that people wear jewellery, art jewellers have used the body in photography as a near inanimate sculpture upon which their own art may work.

On the whole, the photograph of the body and new jewellery have been less concerned with the probing of fears and feelings and more with formal abstraction and fragmentation, for, and this is consistent with one of the many pertinent observations made by Ewing about twentieth-century photography and the body, both art jewellers and photographers share an interest in the abstraction of the human body. In art jewellery this has frequently meant the isolating of a part of the body by means of an artefact, whilst, as Ewing points out, the marked difference between art photography of the ninetieth century and that of the twentieth is in the twentieth-century preoccupation with the fragmenting of the figure to achieve abstract compositions. Time and again, the jewellery catalogues of the last thirty years show that the abstractionist ambitions of the art jewellery and the photographer coincide.

Examples of this are found in the work of Emmy van Leersum, David Watkins and Marjorie Schick. Framing the head or the torso (van Leersum, Gijs Bakker, David Watkins) or building around the head with large light constructions (Marjorie Schick) or draping parts of the body with objects that are half jewellery, half clothing (Lam de Wolf, Caroline Broadhead) are all stratagems for making the human sculpture work in terms of form and volume. The body is treated like a still life.

→ 108
→ 135
→ 131

→ 65

It is surprising, however, given the central role that photography has in Western capitalist societies as a means of selling things, that relatively few catalogues of new jewellery have been successful in selling the idea of new jewellery as an ornament that can reasonably and pleasurably be worn with physical and psychological comfort.

The advantages of photography notwithstanding, many art jewellers want people to wear their work in real life. This means making work that it is possible to wear. Wearability is a design problem and there are several functional aspects such as the nature of the clasps, weight and durability. It also means making work that is possible to wear psychologically. There is a range of values that is still important to the ordinary but visually informed buyer, expressed in a vocabulary that may make art critics shudder but which still has its place in the purpose of jewellery, such as: *pretty, charming, attractive, it suits you, it really matches that dress/suit/ blouse/shirt/your complexion/personality, that's really you* and *I wouldn't be seen dead wearing that.*

Nudity has become such a commonplace motif in advertising that serious photographers believe that some shock therapy is needed in order to reclaim the body for art.

The sceptical critic of new jewellery, if asked "What can be worn?", might be tempted to reply "Anything." After all there is nothing left that one can think of that has not been proposed as jewellery— if not in public, then you can be fairly sure in private. But jewellers themselves, insofar as they are designing for other jewellers or competing with other artists, do not believe that anything goes. If it did, the game would hold no interest. Instead what we see is a really startling series of invented objects. After all, as jewellers know, wearability is not such a difficult function to fulfill. Most materials are acceptable, and size is a matter of what you can persuade your clients to wear. Only weight is the real issue, and there are many solutions to that problem. This the artist (or designer) is more or less free to do what he or she wants.

The body is so obliging: there are blank walls— the torso—and plenty of hooks and ledges, fingers, wrists upper and lower arms, ears, necks, hair ankles and so on.

What remains important, however, is the inner coherence of the design itself. For each object (selected for jewellery of our time) you can discern a critical, aesthetically motivated intelligence—one can infer the judgements and decisions retrospectively by looking at the works, noting the relationships of scale in form, volume and texture, how colour has been used, which of the twentieth-century orthodoxies on design and decoration a piece tends toward and so forth.

The result is a cornucopia of images and forms that shows more variety than has been achieved in the worlds of the museum, gallery or publicly sited sculpture. Within this variety, almost all of the criteria that anyone might wish to list as necessary to the creation of good art are present: some work shows great craft knowledge, some is conceptually clever, some shows concept and craft working together, some of it explores ornamentation, some of it seizes upon contemporary imagery, and other work is classically orientated. All that is holding it together as a body of work is the body. Someone must wear it, but as wearability itself is not a strict taskmaster, the degree to which the body itself is acknowledged as providing both artistic constraints and a subject matter is left up to the individual artist.

And the body is where the art of the jeweller resides. It is frequently only when a piece of jewellery is worn—not posed for a photograph—but used, moving with its wearer, becoming part of the wearer's appearance, that the work can be judged. Jewellery becomes linked with the wearer's identity, with their view of themselves and with how others view them. The bodies that we see in the street or in the office or on the beach are people. The way they move and display themselves is not only a matter of biology and physics but also of psychology. If the work is relatively conventional, there will be those whose conventions and tastes coincide with the jeweller's. But for artists pursuing the extremes, there are some interesting choices. The body can be seen as a soft machine for displaying the art in a photograph, or it can be ignored entirely if the goal is a gallery wall or a showcase. But to pursue the extreme and to want that extreme worn by a person takes a different sort of imagination. It requires an understanding of the psychology of wearing unconventional objects. This understanding is probably quite rare. Perhaps the best "extreme" jewellery is that conceived for a specific person.

Wearability is not a function of market research but a function of imagination in new jewellery. New jewellery may be interesting to look at, but no contemporary jeweller is likely to be bothered by mass appeal. There would be no point. That aspect of wearability is solved more easily and economically by industry. New jewellery is a product of the culture of individualism: there are shared values, but they tend to be shared between individuals within minorities rather than in crowds. This has been the raison d'être of the last thirty-five years of craft or craft-like production of unique objects in an age of mass manufacture.

PAGE 108 · **Gijs Bakker** · *The Tongue* · 1985 · Brooch · Rhodium-plated white gold, silver, diamond, black-and-white photograph, PVC · 115 × 88 × 10 mm

PAGE 109 · **Gijs Bakker** · *Dew Drop* · 1982 · Neck piece · Colour photograph, PVC · 550 × 490 × 1 mm

PAGE 110 · **David Watkins** · *Wing Wave 2* · 1983 · Neck piece · Neoprene-coated wood and steel · 250 × 300 × 4 mm

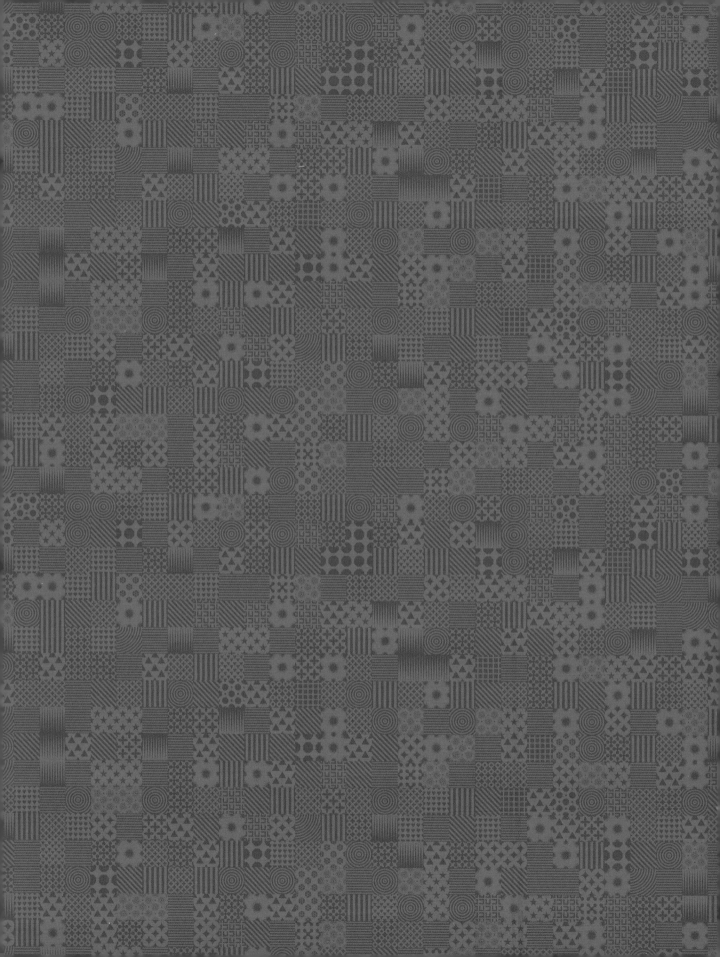

Exhibition

Introduction

Jewellery is often expected to be precious, a luxury item given on a special occasion. A brooch is precious to you because it was chosen for you on your twenty-first birthday or belonged to your grandmother given by a loved one. But the pleasures of jewellery—whether wearing, giving or making—can also be unexpected.

Contemporary jewellers shift the expected values in jewellery. Their inventive ideas find starting points in unusual materials, the joys of making real or imagined scenarios in which jewellery is worn and comes alive. Whether their focus is on the object or a creative system, makers play against jewellery's loaded meanings. They bring attention back to its intrinsic values: preciousness is shown to lie in what jewellery means to people. So despite a maker's intention, jewellery will take on many meanings and speak for its wearer in unpredictable ways. This, for many jewellers, is an unexpected pleasure.

The context of the Design Museum offered the opportunity to think about contemporary jewellery in a different way. I concur with Deyan Sudjic when he says that our relationships to our possessions are never straightforward. Design operates through seduction by object, with a vital recognition of people's needs. Jewellery captures a different sense of "must have": what appears a frivolous luxury will be kept long after other possessions are discarded. *Unexpected Pleasures* explores these links through contemporary jewellery, and focuses on you, the wearer, as an essential part of the creative process.

As both a twentieth-century movement and a flourishing profession, contemporary jewellery has managed to stay vibrant because it is differentiated by certain ways of thinking. The field first appeared on my horizon in the late 1970s. I was immediately drawn to its radical questioning about jewellery's social role and its openly subversive interest in materials and making processes. *Unexpected Pleasures* has given me a chance to revisit key influences of the Contemporary Jewellery Movement, though rather than focus on the work of a select group of makers or present a chronological survey, I have applied a maker's approach to exploring ideas. The process was in no way linear. I relied on an autonomous—even disobedient— consideration of jewellery expressions, finding links that would allow many voices to come to the fore.

The thinking in this exhibition may come as unexpected to the many great jewellers featured within the show and the many great jewellers who could not be fit in. The response for submissions was impressive, and the difficulty in editing large numbers of works to five or six pieces in a limited range of approaches presented its own set of challenges. In chasing objectivity, the links that link works have been uncovered. They are associations by design. And I have always practiced on the field's periphery, pursuing a cross-sectional interest in art, design, jewellery, technology and street subcultures. It was during a stay in Hong Kong that I became aware of a new era of unconscious adornment. The first Walkman was released on the market and every man, woman and child was wearing bright orange foam discs on their ears. They were simply everywhere and I was immediately drawn to their jewellery quality. Aside from an obvious utility, these discs signalled a readiness for private pleasures at the very heart of the public world.

I remain uncertain as to whether it's ego, voyeurism or design thinking that leads to a fixation on the user/wearer. This particular focus underpins an exploration of contemporary jewellery in three sections that follow—*Worn Out*, *Linking Links* and *A Fine Line*. The exhibition presents a cluster of perspectives as a way of understanding the ideas in contemporary jewellery. And each individual cluster within the exhibition offers examples of how works speak to one another, and by doing so positions their makers across a set of creative systems that define what contemporary jewellery means over time. I have chosen not to speak on any individual work, instead to leave its meaning to the imagination of the viewer. By weaving ideas about making, wearing and belonging, it is hoped that people will gain a better understanding of how and why they wear jewellery.

New conversations between makers and wearers should generate new thinking about contemporary jewellery. I could not have pre-imagined how this exhibition would evolve or the conversations that have led to its solution. The result is unexpected, which is, of course, the point.

→ 116
→ 156
→ 210

CHAPTER FOUR

Worn Out

Worn Out enlivens the exhibition by highlighting the different ways contemporary jewellery is worn. After all, jewellery needs to be worn by real people in real situations to realise its full potential. Along with our clothing, sunglasses and wearable technologies, jewellery will say where we belong in the world. It will express intent, add detail to our daily rituals, signal an inner life and, of course, invite the viewer to read between the lines. Jewellery will attach itself to its wearer, making either discreet intimate connections or bolder public statements. It can be serious or frivolous, experimental or ceremonial, tasteful or daring, but in all circumstances jewellery will "talk" for its wearer.

For contemporary jewellers, imagining how jewellery adorns the body is part of a creative process centred in design and art practice. Here, this section offers a selection of bolder statements that exemplify this single proposition, giving an insight into past experimentation as well as current thinking by mixing significant pieces from the Contemporary Jewellery Movement with a range of exciting new works. And if you are lucky enough to wear one of these extravagant pieces, it may be surprising how carefully wearing has been considered in making, and how much pleasure is experienced when "worn out".

WORN OUT NOW

 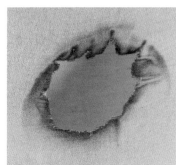 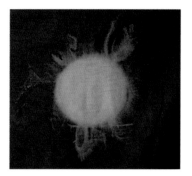

LEFT AND OPPOSITE · **Monika Brugger** · *Rouge (Red)* · 2001 · Brooch · Linen and cotton dress · 1,290–1,340 mm long

CENTRE AND OPPOSITE · **Monika Brugger** · *Brandal (Mark by Fire)* · 2001 · Brooch · Linen and cotton dress · 1,290–1,340 mm long

RIGHT AND OPPOSITE · **Monika Brugger** · *Soleil (Sun)* · 2001 · Brooch · Linen and cotton dress · 1,290–1,340 mm long

Susanne Klemm · *Frozen* · 2007 · Neck piece · Polyolefin · 450 × 450 × 60 mm

Lucy Sarneel · *Mourning Piece* · 2008 · Bib · Antique textiles on rubber, silver, thread, zinc · 390 × 210 × 22 mm

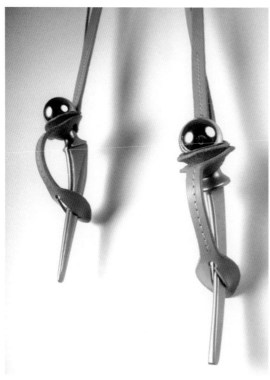

OPPOSITE · **Sari Liimatta** · *Phoenix* · 2010 ·
Neck piece · Glass beads, pins, oxidised silver, a plastic toy · 450 × 80 × 60 mm

TOP · **Christoph Zellweger** · *Relic Rosé* · 2007/2008 ·
Neckpiece · mixed media, silver, flock · various sizes

LEFT · **Christoph Zellweger** · *Hip Piece* · 2002 ·
Pendant · Second-hand hip replacement, medical steel, leather · 500 mm length

ABOVE · **Beverley Price** · *Nespresso Collar* · 2008–9 ·

Neck piece · Nespresso capsules recycled, anodised wire, and jewellers' binding wire · 360 × 35 mm

OPPOSITE · **Marjorie Schick** · *Spiralling Discs (32 necklaces and bracelets)* · 2006 ·

Neck pieces, bracelets · Painted wood · From 305 mm diameter x 13 mm to 127 mm diameter x 13 mm

Lisa Walker · *Playmobile Necklace* · 2010 · Neck piece · Plastic, thread · 350 mm diameter

Florian Ladstätter · *Rope Necklace* · 2007 · Necklace · Cast resin, cord · Rope fittings: 71 × 42 × 17.5 mm; necklace: 900 × 650 × 17.5 mm

Dorothea Prühl · *Hawk* · 2006 · Neck piece · Elm wood · 400 mm height

Tota Reciclados · *Theorie du Champ Mechanique* · 2010

Neck piece · Found objects: book covers, textiles, metal, glass, clay, enamel wood, pearls · 220 × 530 mm

WORN OUT ORIGINS

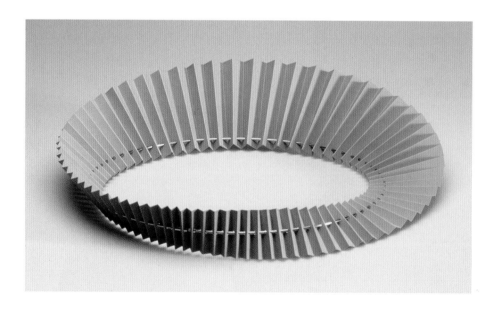

ABOVE · **Paul Derrez** · *Pleated Collar* · 1982 · Neck piece · Plastic, steel · 850 mm diameter

OPPOSITE · **Marjorie Schick** · *Azo Orange* · 1986 · Neck piece · Painted wood · 527 × 584 x 254 mm diameter

OPPOSITE · **Therese Hilbert** · *Red Neckpiece* · 1983 · Neck piece · Brass, varnished red PVC, steel · 450 × 430 mm

ABOVE · **Bernhard Schobinger** · *Bottlenecklace* · 1980 · Necklace · Broken-off bottlenecks, metal cord · 370 mm diameter

ABOVE · **Gijs Bakker** · *Dew Drop* · 1982 · Neck piece · Colour photograph, PVC · 550 × 490 × 1 mm

OPPOSITE · **David Watkins** · *Atoll* · 1985 · Neck piece · Neoprene on wood and steel · 410 × 315 × 4 mm

CHAPTER FIVE

Worn Out Photography

Contemporary jewellers have always used portrait and scenario photography to show how ordinary men and women wear jewellery. However, photography has become more than mere documentary tool: it has also become a pivotal mode of expression and a key device for experimentation with ideas. In the photograph contemporary jewellery is removed from the gallery space, the maker's studio or collector's drawer, and it can be shown as an aesthetic fantasy, an imaginary proposition, a poetic association or a simple narrative.

This section shows photographs featuring some of the most uninhibited works from different times in contemporary jewellery practice. The images are divided into three parts—"Jewellery as Object", "Body", "Propositions"—each highlighting different tactics and thoughts about what jewellery is or could be. Looking at the odd assortment of images here, together they reveal that jewellery propositions are rarely just jewellery. These propositions rely on people, even when jewellery's wearability is stretched to extremes or the idea talks about jewellery in a symbolic way. Photography allows jewellers to experiment with ideas about jewellery and to sample from the wider world around them, suggesting there will always be an ongoing conversation across those fine lines between art, craft and design.

Jewellery as Object

Photography has come to play an increasingly significant role for contemporary jewellery. It can document fleeting experiments. It can take the place of the work or even become it when an ephemeral object disappears. Photography can be used to observe the way in which jewellery is worn, and as in the case of Maisie Maud Broadhead, it can explore the place of jewellery in art practice. Broadhead, who studied jewellery at the Royal College of Art, has produced a series of images that focus on historical works of art in which jewellery forms a key part of the subject matter. She makes a version of the jewellery then photographs it in a re-creation of the original painting. *Allegory of Wealth*, by Simon Vouet, a pioneer of French baroque, dates from 1640. In Broadhead's version, the necklace held by a winged cherub is a string of sweets. South African–born Beverley Price takes a political view of gold given its part in the colonial history of the country. She questions the nature of its value, plating humble found objects with the material. In Andy Gut's case, the surreal image of the brooch apparently sprouting like an organic growth from the body is a key to understanding the maker's intentions. Bernhard Schobinger's work is photographed by his wife in black and white, with the work worn by his daughter. Mah Rana was commissioned by the MIMA gallery in Middlesbrough to produce Meanings and Attachments. Her photographs documented local people and the significance of jewellery to them. Carlier Makigawa and Therese Hilbert both use monochrome photographic images to capture the essence of their work.

ABOVE · **Maisie Broadhead** · *Sweet Necklace* · 2010 ·
Necklace · Sweets · Approximately 200 × 200 mm
OPPOSITE · **Maisie Broadhead** · *Keep Them Sweet* · 2010 ·
Photograph · Digital C-type print · 1,450 × 1,065 mm

OPPOSITE · **Beverley Price** · *All Gold is Gold* · 2005–6 · Photograph · Fine gold, 750 gold,
aluminium, plastic, images of "all gold" jam, wire (Small platelets—two necklaces) · 370 × 200 mm
ABOVE · **Andy Gut** · *Hirsch* · 2006 · Photograph · Nylon, titanium · 25 × 70 × 25 mm

 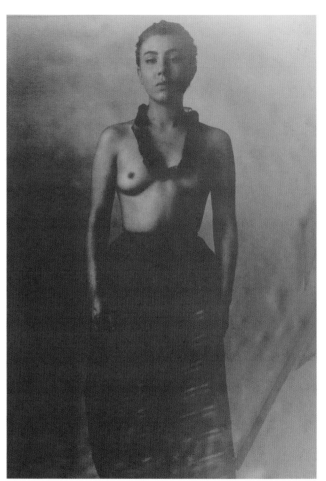

ABOVE LEFT · **Annelies Štrba / Bernhard Schobinger** · *Sonja with Necklace* · 1988 ·

Photograph · Photograph on paper · 305 × 235 mm

ABOVE RIGHT · **Annelies Štrba / Bernhard Schobinger** · *Sonja with bottleneck* · 1988 ·

Photograph · Photograph on paper · 305 × 235 mm

Mah Rana · *Meanings and Attachments: I Made This Bracelet Myself and I Wear It Quite a Lot. I Like Big Colours and Things. Amy and Kyle* · 2006 · Calendar · g2 photography · Various sizes

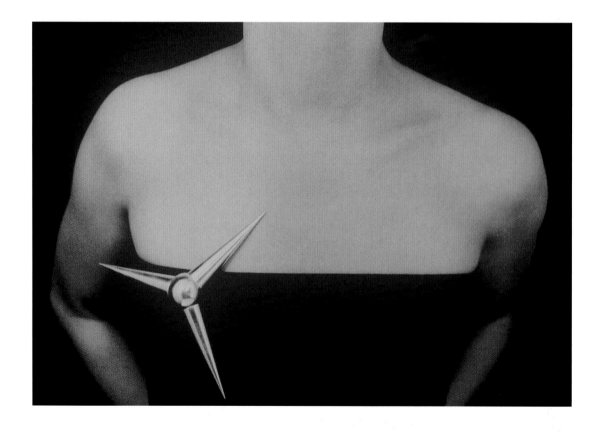

ABOVE · **Therese Hilbert** · *Star* · 1985 · Photograph · Star: 150 × 125 × 32 mm

OPPOSITE · **Carlier Makigawa** · *Brooch* · 1991 · Photograph · Repoussé silver, monel · 170 × 40 × 25 mm

Body

When Gerd Rothmann asks us to think about why we consider adorning the ear but not the nose, it is through a photograph, just as David Watkins's elegant framing of the torso is best delineated by a photographic image. Tiffany Parbs explores the limits of body alterations with her work with hair extensions for the eyelashes and the disturbing blister ring, while Norman Cherry illustrates the aesthetic potential of tissue engineering for growing body extensions.

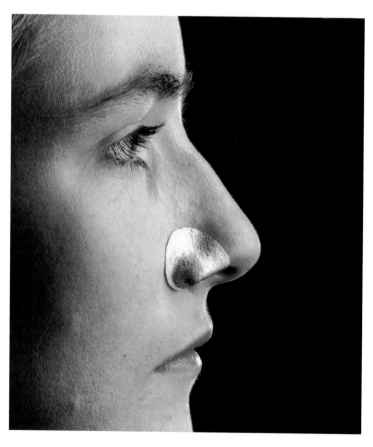

ABOVE · **Gerd Rothmann** · *Nostril* · 1985 ·

Photograph · Gold · Nose piece: size 15 × 15 × 6 mm

OPPOSITE · **David Watkins** · *Interlocking Bodypiece 2* · 1976 ·

Photograph · Steel · 500 × 400 × 100 mm when collapsed

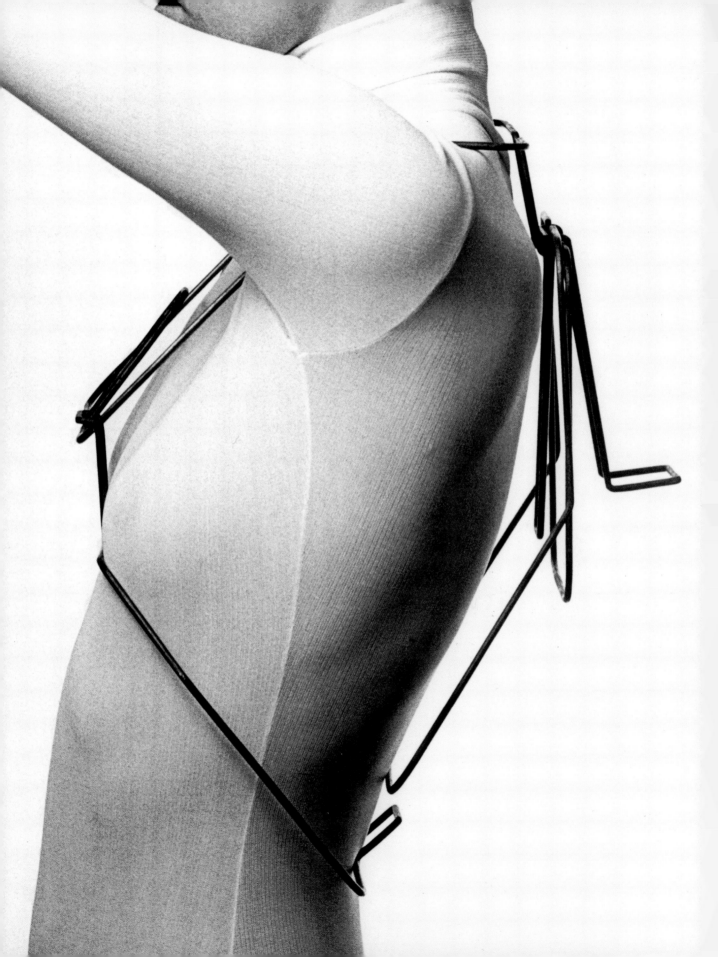

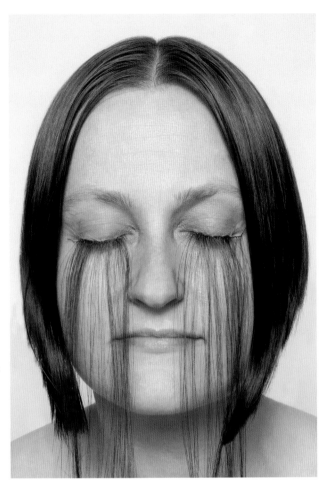

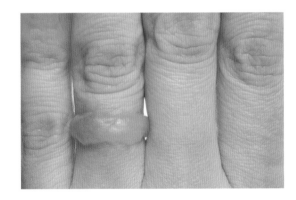

ABOVE LEFT · **Tiffany Parbs** · *Extension* · 2008 ·
Photograph · Hand-woven hair, digital print · 470 × 330 × 35 mm
ABOVE RIGHT · **Tiffany Parbs** · *Blister Ring* · 2005 ·
Photograph · Skin, digital print · 330 × 470 × 35 mm

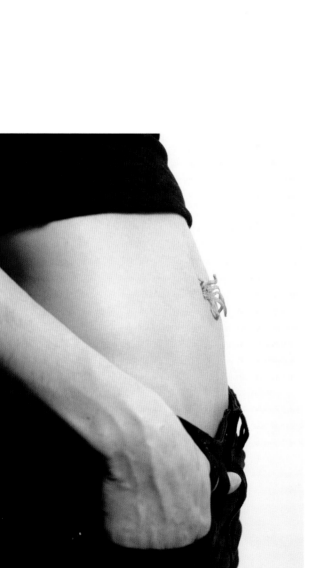

ABOVE · **Norman Cherry** · *Katherine* · 2004
Photograph · Digital print · Various sizes
LEFT · **Norman Cherry** · *Shadi* · 2008/9
Photograph · Digital print · Various sizes

Propositions

Photography is a powerful way of exploring the question of what constitutes jewellery. Each succeeding generation is ready to look for new definitions. Susan Pietzsch and Valentina Seidel's image is suggesting that we may be adorning our cars in ways which suggest jewellery, or even that the car itself might constitute jewellery. Suska Mackert uses text in a site-specific work with photography to comment ironically on the qualities of jewellery. Ursula de Guttmann's lumps seem to erupt through clothing as an extension of the body, just as Gijs Bakker's clothing suggestions change the profile of the body or use photography to imply the body underneath. Otto Künzli's *Beauty Gallery* is a provocation, using picture frames to ask us to reconsider the purposes of adornment.

ABOVE AND OPPOSITE · **Suska Mackert** · *Wrappinghood* · 2005 ·
Site-specific work · Digital print, gold-leaf letters · 100 mm height

<u>ABOVE</u> · **Susan Pietzsch & Valentina Seidel** · *Spring Summer '07 Crystals* · 2007 · Photograph · Digital print · 600 × 400 mm

A Small Deposit Secures Any Item

MATERIALS WITH A SHINY SURFACE
REFLECT LIGHT, WHILE ELSEWHERE
THE LIGHT IS FULLY ABSORBED

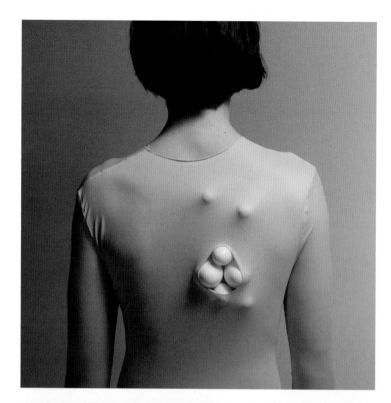

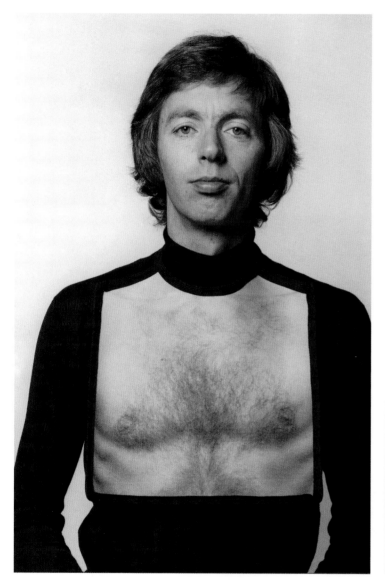

OPPOSITE TOP · **Ursula Guttmann** · *(x) : tension_1* · 2010 · Photograph · T-shirt, silicone, steel · 1,000 × 400 × 800 mm

OPPOSITE BOTTOM · **Ursula Guttmann** · *(x) : tension_2* · 2010 · Photograph · T-shirt, silicone, steel · 1,000 × 400 × 800 mm

ABOVE LEFT · **Gijs Bakker** · *Bib / Slab* · 1976 · Photograph · Photograph, linen, cotton · Bib size: 330 × 320 × 3 mm

ABOVE RIGHT · **Gijs Bakker with Emmy van Leersum** · *Clothing Suggestions* · 1970 · Clothing · Polyester knitting

in the round, nylon (manufacture: Tiny Leeuwenkamp) · Various sizes

ABOVE, RIGHT AND OPPOSITE · **Otto Künzli** · *Beauty Gallery* ·

1984 · Photography · Cibachrome PS · 750 × 625 mm

OPPOSITE · *Kiki*

TOP LEFT · *Andrea*

TOP RIGHT · *Uschi*

BOTTOM LEFT · *Gina*

BOTTOM RIGHT · *Susy*

CHAPTER SIX

Linking Links

Linking Links looks at the way meaning is invested and expressed in contemporary jewellery. Social networks and the environment in which jewellers work conditions their thinking, shaping their ideas about making, wearing and belonging. Contemporary jewellers inventively play with creative strategies to make their artistic statements, opening up not only links between different media but also unexpected links between people.

Here, jewellery objects are clustered according to ideas and approaches that bridge the experiences of both the maker and the wearer. Using themes as a structure to link seemingly disparate works, each individual cluster is collected into one of two streams of thinking: the first focusing on the creative systems in which jewellery is made, and the second highlighting the social expressions used in jewellery to express belonging.

Each cluster offers examples of how works will speak to one another, while the conversation between clusters draws specific attention to the key forces that drive jewellery's production and use. At the centre of this conversation lies design thinking, and this section highlights those aspects of design that are central to contemporary-jewellery practice, including aesthetics, materiality, technology and reproduction.

The clustering of works in Linking Links invites a sweep of focus, from the micro scale—where the enduring qualities of jewellery are laid bare—to the macro scale, where the meanings are opened to imaginative interpretation. And an opportunity is presented to begin an understanding of the broader "creative" language of contemporary jewellery.

LOGICAL SOLUTIONS

One recurring theme in contemporary jewellery is the use of logic for a system of components. When adapted to jewellery, industrial materials and processes can be used not for conventional mass production but to create standardised jewellery forms and elements. Makers exploit repetition to introduce subtle differences in each individual piece of jewellery, such as **Sue Lorraine's** water-jet-cut mild-steel *Petal* brooches. With *White Forms*, **Marc Monzó** has made a set of nylon components that wearers can configure to their own specifications. **Camilla Prasch** has taken a simple snap fastener and attached it to a set of silicone discs to make a bracelet, while **Manon van Kouswijk** has made a necklace from adhesive paper dots.

Another tactic is to reference machine-made mechanisms, such as **Blanche Tilden's** bicycle chain, and interpret their system as jewellery. Sometimes, a maker offers an unexpected logic, as in *Chew Your Own Brooch* by **Ted Noten**, which delegates the designer's role to the wearer. Individual designs are created by chewing gum, and the results are then cast in silver, gold-plated, and mounted on a pin.

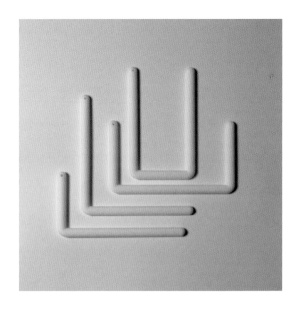

Marc Monzó · *White Form* · 2010 · Brooch · Nylon · 95 × 70 mm

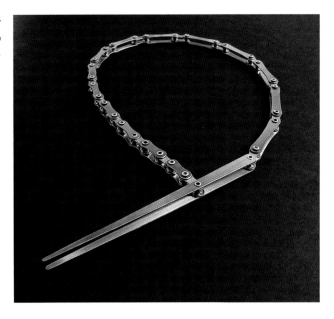

Blanche Tilden · *Speed* · 2000 · Neck piece ·
Borosilicate glass, titanium, anodised aluminium · 12 × 240 mm

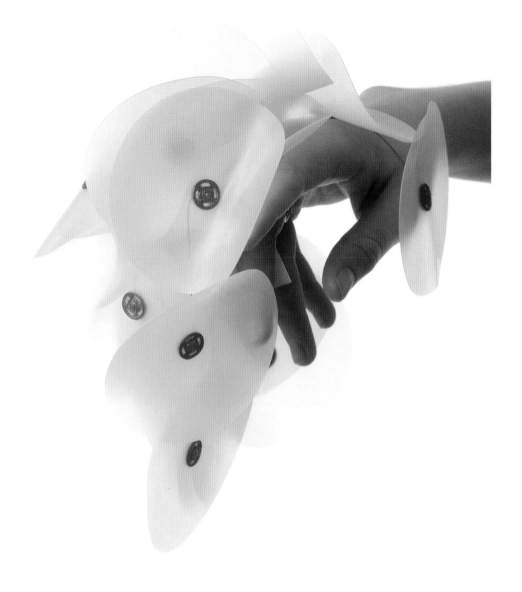

Camilla Prasch · *MEGA* · 2009 · Ring ·

Red dyed snap fasteners, nylon thread, silicone discs · 310 × 110 mm

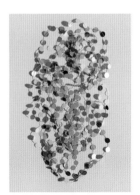

Ted Noten → 38

Ted Noten → 38

Manon van Kouswijk → 39

Sue Lorraine → 40

ALSO IN THIS CLUSTER

MULTIPLE ORIGINALS

By playing with making processes, jewellers create unique objects that, nevertheless, can be made in multiples. Repetition provides a starting point for experimentation, with minor variations on a single theme creating differences. **Shunichiro Nakashima** employs thread, mainly silk, in which feathers have been twisted to make a family of brightly coloured pieces of jewellery. They read as a group, but each is different. *Ashanti* is **Johanna Dahm's** name for a series of rings made using the more traditional method of lost-wax casting. The mould can only be used once, and each ring is slightly different because the moulding process cannot be precisely controlled. **Lucy Sarneel's** *Leaf* pins use zinc sheet, an industrial material, with hand making.

Three other examples are **Esther Knobel's** *Variations on a Rose* brooches, which capture dried roses, fruit and chewing gum in silver stalks; **Marian Hosking's** use of organic materials to create multiple forms, in her case shell shards; and **Sally Marsland's** use of epoxy resin to make multicoloured flowers.

Lucy Sarneel · *Leaf Pins* · 1998–ongoing ·
Pins · Zinc · Various sizes

Johanna Dahm · *Ashanti* · 1998–2003 · Rings · 750 yellow gold
hollow cast in the technique of the Asanti in Ghana · Approx. 30 × 30 × 120 mm

Shunichiro Nakashima · *Maki Series* · 2004–2006 · Brooches, earrings, bangles ·

Silk, wool, linen, cotton, rayon, paper, gold, foil, feather · Various sizes

Sally Marsland → 41   Esther Knobel → 41   Marian Hosking → 41

ALSO IN THIS CLUSTER

NEGATIVE SPACE

Sometimes the spirit of a jewellery piece lies in the relationship between the object and the space it occupies. The significance of its form is enhanced by what is absent, its negative space exerting an equal positive charge. Often work, such as that by **Ramón Puig Cuyàs**, will carry an architectural quality, its design expressing the cultural character of its maker. **Simon Cottrell's** brooch constructed from stainless-steel sheet is more volumetric, while **Katja Prins's** *Continuum* brooch has more mechanical associations. It can be surprising to see how a work will change when worn on different bodies. Also reflecting this idea of negative space are **Susie Ganch's** brooch made from a cluster of rings; **Fabrizio Tridenti's** brooch with a more organic quality and made from painted silver and brass; and **Jiro Kamata's** combination of a ready-made camera lens with oxidised silver mounts.

Simon Cottrell · *Four Barrelled Drops Focused* · 2011 ·
Brooch · 80 × 60 × 40 mm

Katja Prins · *Continuum Brooch* · 2010 · Brooch ·
Silver, sealing wax, silicone rubber · 76 × 65 × 26 mm

162

Ramón Puig Cuyàs · *No. 1359 Brooch (Subtle Architectures Series)* · 2010

Brooch · Nickel, oxidised silver · 75 × 70 × 20 mm

Susie Ganch → 42

Jiro Kamata → 43

Fabrizio Tridenti → 43

ALSO IN THIS CLUSTER

PHYSICAL MATTERS

Materiality is an essential aspect of much jewellery; paper, silver and wood all have their own special allure. Each brings emotional associations, and the maker works to bring out the essence of the substance. Material qualities—tactility, colour, weight, surface and so on—will enhance an idea, add an ambiguous quality or simply express the personality of the maker. **Rut-Malin Barklund** takes paper as the starting point for a neck piece, compacting it to express compression. **Kazumi Nagano** also uses paper, but here the reference is to the Japanese history of pleating material. **Christine Graf** is more ambiguous: she works with a mix of materials, such as copper, enamel, gold and patinated silver. At first sight it is not entirely clear what her pieces are made from, but despite this, the material quality of the piece leaves a lasting impression. Variations on this theme include work by **Warwick Freeman**, who makes the material quality of his screwdriver handles in lava and stone communicate as strongly as their obvious phallic references; **Helen Britton's** brooch made from painted silver and jagged shards of glass, which is still more aggressive; and **John Iverson**, who builds up the surface of his brooch with shaped fragments.

Kazumi Nagano · *Untitled* · 2009 · Brooch ·
Japanese paper, gold, silver pin, nylon thread and
Japanese lacquer · 95 × 95 × 53 mm

Christine Graf · *Green Rain* · 2010 · Brooch · Copper mesh, enamel,
gold, patinated silver, nylon thread, stainless steel pin · 86 × 95 × 30 mm

Rut-Malin Barklund · *Paper Series* · 2010

Neck piece · Paper, silver · 100 × 40 mm, length of chain 200 mm

Helen Britton → 44   John Iversen → 44   Warwick Freeman → 45

ALSO IN THIS CLUSTER

HAND-MADE

To invest the time and skill needed to construct something by hand suggests it has been made with personal commitment. When wearing a handmade piece of contemporary jewellery, it can feel like an invitation to connect with the maker. Hand making combines an idea with an aesthetic quality. It sometimes takes on an aspect of alchemy, whether in the intricate precision of the enamelling of **Helen Aitken-Kuhnen's** beach brooches or in **Nel Linssen's** necklace, which is made from the painstaking folding into three-dimensional fragments of an apparently endless stack of paper discs. The colour finish turns the seemingly solid whole into a shimmering object.

Another form of handwork is visible in the crocheting of **Jungjung Itomika**, who produced a broccoli textile brooch with a startling level of realism and skill. Hand making is also a powerful vehicle for conveying the specificities of particular cultures. **Gabriela Horvat's** wool-and-silk rope piece looks crude, but it is actually a highly refined reference to the traditions of Argentina and is in sharp contrast to **Yutaka Minegishi's** finely honed bone and ebony rings.

Helen Aitken-Kuhnen · *Beach Brooches* · 2010
Brooches · Sterling silver, enamel · 9 × 2.8 mm

Nel Linssen · *Necklace* · 2009
Necklace · Plastic-covered paper · section 23 mm; height 20 mm

Jungjung Itomika · *Broccoli* · 2010 · Brooch · Cotton crochet thread · 40 × 50 mm

Yutaka Minegishi → 45   Yutaka Minegishi → 45   Nel Linssen → 46   Gabriela Horvat → 47

ALSO IN THIS CLUSTER

QUIRKY IDEAS

Over time, jewellery makers establish an artistic identity through their work, adopting a distinctive signature which can be used to articulate a perspective on contemporary jewellery. What might seem like a quirky idea can reflect a distinctive persona, highlighting an idiosyncratic individual approach to making jewellery. The work on this page is from a number of highly experienced jewellers, people who over the years have had the chance to reflect on the nature of their work, to find their own voice and to respond to developments in jewellery. **Robert Baines's** red and green electroplated silver is one of a number of examples of pieces of what might be called jewellery-like objects, which seem to lose their intimate connection with the body. **Philip Sajet** is a highly skilled enameller and goldsmith. **Daniel Kruger**, from South Africa, works with lapis lazuli and glass beads. All three have developed a personal signature—as have **Georg Dobler** with his insect forms, **Ruudt Peters** with his phallic symbols, and **Fritz Maierhofer** with his expressive language.

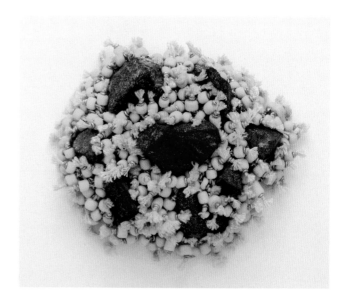

Daniel Kruger · *Brooch* · 2002

Brooch · Lapis lazuli, glass beads, textile, silver · 30 × 70 × 80 mm

Philip Sajet · *A La Recherche de Joyou Perdu* · 2011 · Rings ·

Gold, enamel, silver, amethyst, rock crystal · ring 1: 56 mm height; ring 2: 53 mm height

Robert Baines · *Redder Than Green* · 2009 · Brooch ·

Silver, powdercoat, paint, collected object, electroplate · 123 × 93 × 63 mm

Georg Dobler → 48

Ruudt Peters → 49

Fritz Maierhofer → 49

ALSO IN THIS CLUSTER

MODERNIST SPIRIT

Whilst contemporary jewellery has thrived in our postmodern world, modernist ideas are still important to many jewellers. Some of them are not comfortable with postmodernism's willfulness, and they have continued to develop their signature using the aesthetics of modernism. Simple, clean lines and an absence of decorative detailing underpin the power of this kind of work. **Johannes Kuhnen** goes as far as to refer to the modern movement's interest in modular components with his interchangeable pendant system. Mark Edgoose's ring, constructed from niobium, has the presence of sculpture on a miniature scale, and it forms part of a stand that holds the ring when it is not being worn. **Therese Hilbert's** brooch is made from silver formed to leave no traces of the maker's hand, in typical modernist fashion. **Yong-il Jeon** reflects a similar sensibility from the Korean perspective, and Warwick Freeman's *Lattice* and Beppe Kessler's *Timeless* are based on an equally restrained geometry.

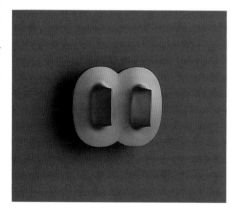

Yong-il Jeon · *Passage 1* · 2007 ·
Brooch · 750 gold · 39 × 51 × 21 mm

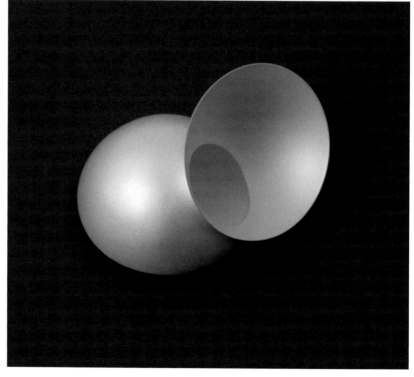

Therese Hilbert · *Brooch* · 2005 · Silver · 27 × 54 × 54 mm

Johannes Kuhnen · *Interchangeable Pendant System* · 2000

Pendants · Anodised aluminium, stainless steel, .925 silver · 50 × 50 mm

Beppe Kessler → 50

Mark Edgoose → 51

Warwick Freeman → 51

ALSO IN THIS CLUSTER

ANYTHING GOES

Just as the originators of the contemporary jewellery movement produced work that set out to disrupt conventional views of what constituted jewellery, so a younger generation has also set out to make work that transgresses what have now become conventions. **Andy Gut** plays with ideas of what is wearable and what is not. In comparison with **Mia Maljojoki's** plaster object, dangling from a twisted rubber band, Gut's twig-like pieces are surprisingly accommodating. Some jewellers pay serious attention to play. Others, such as **Nicholas Bastin**, with the intriguingly titled *Crayfish Reconstruction*, sidestep the sense of refinement associated with jewellery and adopt an anything-goes mentality. They celebrate colour and plasticity, using materials in an exuberant and seemingly uncontrolled way. In doing so, they invite us to play along with them as they break the rules. **Noon Passama** used gold-plated brass to support a fur tassel put to work as a brooch; **Maud Traon's** ring is a varnished-foam-and-putty object that appears willfully ugly. **Adam Paxon's** brooch with four eyes is more obviously engaging.

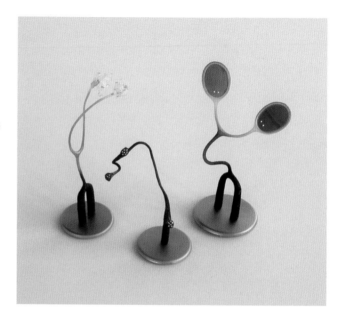

Andy Gut · *Mimesen* · 2006 · Brooches ·
Nylon, titanium, diamonds, gold · Each approx. 25 × 70 × 25 mm

Nicholas Bastin · *Crayfish Reconstruction (Section 7)* · 2009 · Brooch ·
Sterling silver, stainless steel, polyurethane resin, epoxy resin · 75 × 60 × 50 mm

Mia Maljojoki · Necklace from the series *Explosive: Frozen Fireworks* ·

2011 · Necklace · Plaster, pigment, paint, garnet, string · 120 × 500 × 40 mm

Adam Paxon → 52

Maud Traon → 52

Noon Passama → 53

ALSO IN THIS CLUSTER

SECOND LIFE

Our society has adopted recycling as a kind of mantra, using it as a symbolic expression of anxiety about overconsumption as a practical means to reduce our use of scarce resources. Many contemporary jewellers reflect on these current concerns in their work. Through regenerating objects and salvaging materials, jewellers inventively create a new kind of preciousness by giving a second life to what would otherwise be discarded as debris. **Mark Vaarwerk's** bracelets transform humble materials— plastic milk cartons and ice cream containers—and team them with silver. **Willy Van de Velde**, with his *White Cross* necklace, highlights the aesthetic and material qualities of everyday objects, such as plastic ties and face masks. **Karl Fritsch's** ring is autobiographical. He was building a house when he put together a cluster of nails and screws. **Taweesak Molsawat's** brooch is the product of collecting fragments washed up on a beach in Thailand and assembling them to tell a narrative. **Sally Marsland** took fragments from a deconstructed eggcup and made them into a pendant.

Mark Vaarwek · *Paul's Bracelet II* · 2008 ·
Bracelet · Plastic Paul's milk bottles, sterling silver · 90 mm

Mark Vaarwek · *Wendy's Bracelet II* · 2008 ·
Bracelet · Plastic Wendy's ice cream topping bottles,
plastic shopping bags, sterling silver · 93 mm

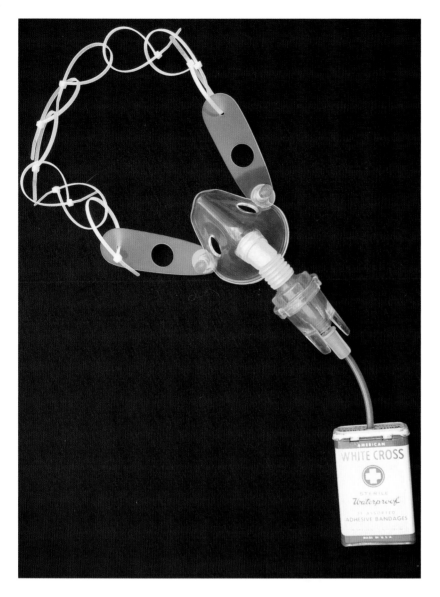

Willy Van de Velde · *White Cross* · 2009 · Neck piece ·
Old box, mask, Plexiglas, plastic straps · 500 × 180 mm

Taweesak Molsawat → 54   Karl Fritsch → 55   Sally Marsland → 55

ALSO IN THIS CLUSTER

FINISH ME OFF

Experimentation with new materials and techniques now extends into the digital world. As these technologies become part of everyday experience, the dexterous hand of the maker can give way to technical processes of reproduction. Jewellers, like product designers, artists and architects, have become interested in the potential of rapid prototyping, as demonstrated by **Gilbert Riedelbauch's** brooch. David Watkins's bracelet uses a more mature form of fabrication—laser cutting—which also questions the nature of handcraft skills. **Doug Bucci**, a diabetic, used 3-D printing to fabricate a neck piece that reflects the patterns of blood sugar in his body. The architect and designer **Ron Arad's** *Not Made By Hand* bracelet speaks for itself. Gijs Bakker's *Porsche* bracelet and Svenja John's more colourful bracelet are both made from polycarbonate.

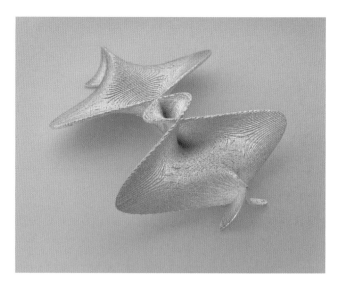

Gilbert Riedelbauch · *CSH Brooch* · 2001 ·

Brooch · Sterling silver · 11.5 × 66.4 × 52.9 mm

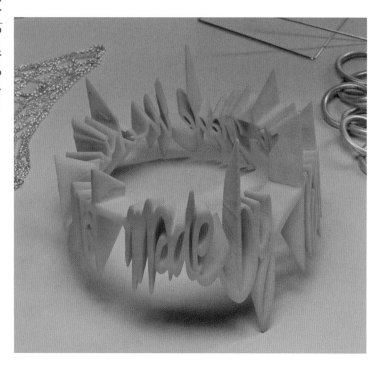

Ron Arad · *Not Made by Hand* · 2002 · Bracelet · Polyamide · 75 × 100mm

Doug Bucci · *Trans-Hematopoietic Neckpiece* · 2010 · Neck piece ·
3-D printed acrylic resin printed as one interlinked piece · 457 × 457 × 51 mm

ALSO IN THIS CLUSTER

INDUSTRIAL VIEWS

Design and industrial production have always sat on the edge of the horizon for contemporary jewellery. They offer a perspective that opens up fresh ways of thinking about how jewellery connects to popular culture. **Simone LeAmon's** bowling arm is a bracelet put together from offcut leather strips, a by-product in the manufacture of cricket balls. **Ted Noten's** series of brooches is cut from the body of a single Mercedes. In fact, one client was so taken with the idea that he commissioned Noten to make a special brooch cut from his own car, so creating an object that adorns both wearer and, through its absence, the vehicle. **Lin Cheung's** tape measure looks like a commercial product, but it adds names to all the significant relationships that we might have in the course of a lifetime, from friend and lover to enemy. The form of the bracelet by **Bless** is that of a basic digital watch, but the material is wood. **Gijs Bakker's** bracelet is a production piece based on a vacuum-formed circle that has been made in its hundreds since it was originally designed in the 1960s.

Simone LeAmon · *Bowling Arm* · 2000 · Bangles · Leather: cricket ball waste · 80 × 90 mm

Gijs Bakker · *Circle in Circle* · 1967 (design); 1989 (remade) · Bracelet · White or smoked Perspex · 118 x 60 mm · Made by Chi ha paura…?

Bless · *Watch bangle* · 2005 · Bracelet · Ebony wood · 85 x 85 x 0.4 mm · Made by Chi ha paura…?

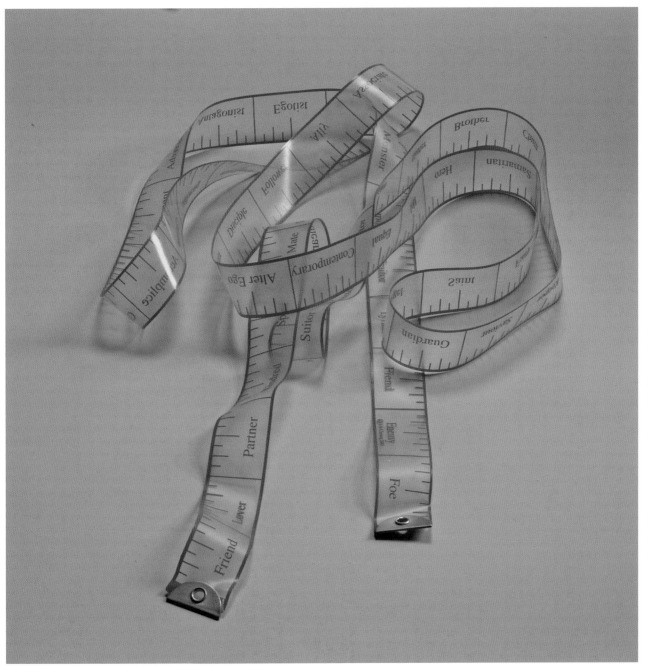

Lin Cheung · *Friend or Foe* · 2007 · Necklace ·
Transparent PVC · 1,400 × 17 mm · Made by Chi ha paura…?

Ted Noten → 58–59

Ted Noten → 59

ALSO IN THIS CLUSTER

SINGLES

The eight works in the next four pages cover the range of approaches and ideas documented in the clusters sections. They range from the chillingly disturbing to the winsome. **Mari Funaki's** work carries an architectural quality, the elements folding into each other to highlight its structural form. **Sigurd Bronger** has translated his passion for machines and instruments into a series of wearable constructions, such as his *Carrying Device for a Goose Egg*. **Robert Smit** has always argued for artistic conceptions in jewellery, and his painterly interpretations in gold became a crucial turning point for rethinking the use of materials in contemporary jewellery. *Rings for Woman in an Armchair*, by **Wendy Ramshaw**, interprets a portrait by Picasso. Her ring towers are both a classic signature and a means for emotional interpretation. By contrast, **Peter Chang** conjures up brightly coloured abstractions made from plastic fragments of existing objects, such as toys and toothbrushes. His complex forms with luscious surfaces are reminiscent of surrealist fantasies.

   Bernhard Schobinger's *Holiday in Cambodia* is not a comfortable object to possess, let alone to wear as a bracelet, despite the beauty of its craftsmanship. It is political in its intent. There is a sombre tradition in jewellery of the memento mori. **Ted Noten's** *Tiara for Maxima* is political in another way. It's a reflection of the way in which the contemporary Dutch state sees itself as open to mildly subversive creative ideas. A competition was held to create a tiara for the new Dutch crown prince's bride, Princess Maxima. Given the prince's known enthusiasm for biking, Noten used the form of a motorcycle helmet, from which the tiara was cut.

Mari Funaki · *Ring* · 2009 · Ring · 20k gold · 25 × 24 × 11 mm
SEE MORE of the **NEGATIVE SPACE** cluster → **162**

Mari Funaki · *Bracelet* · 2009 · Bracelet · Heat-coloured mild steel · 105 × 115 × 45 mm

SEE MORE of the **NEGATIVE SPACE** cluster → **162**

Robert Smit · *Neck Ornament* · 1991 · Neck piece · Gold, paint

SEE MORE of the TURNING POINTS cluster → 204

Ted Noten · *Tiara for Maxima* · 2002 · Tiara · Chrome-plated plastic · 220 mm diameter

SEE MORE of the **CROWNING MOMENT** cluster → **190**

Sigurd Bronger · *Goose Egg Ring* · 1997 · Ring · Steel, silver-gilt, silver, rubber, egg · 60 × 40 mm

SEE MORE of the **QUIRKY IDEAS** cluster → **168**

Bernhard Schobinger · *Holiday in Cambodia II* · 2011 · Bangle · Silver · 98 × 70 mm

SEE MORE of the **MODUS OPERANDI** cluster → 196

ABOVE · **Peter Chang** · *Bracelet* · 2007/2008 ·
Bracelet · Resin, acrylic, silver · 146 × 159 × 70 mm
SEE MORE of the **PHYSICAL MATTERS** cluster → **164**

OPPOSITE · **Wendy Ramshaw** · *Rings for Woman in an Armchair* · 1998 ·
Rings · 750 yellow gold, amethyst, fire opal and citrine on painted wood stands · 200 × 70 mm
SEE MORE of the **MULTIPLE ORIGINALS** cluster → **160**

HEART FELT

Underlying the language of jewellery are a number of universally understood symbols that can represent or trigger emotions. No symbol is more potent or more often used by jewellers than the heart, the token of love. There are many ways that it can be used aside from the obvious one. As part of a series of pieces exploring these emotions, **Constanze Schreiber** worked fine silver to create a heart pendant, *In Memoriam I*, which embodied the sense of the loss of a loved one through the delicate incorporation of a skull. Another in the same series, *Mourning*, created from plastics, wrinkled the surface of the heart, hinting at putrefaction and decay. **Otto Künzli's** *One Centimeter of Love* offers a witty, elegant way for the wearer to express the precise extent of his or her feelings. The heart is cut from a gold extrusion and is available in any length. The heart form lends itself to a range of materials. **Bruce Metcalf** uses richly painted wood for his *Speaking Heart*, while **Otto Künzli** lacquers hard foam for oversize heart brooches. **Iris Eichenberg's** alarmingly literal representations of hearts trailing arteries are made from knitted wool.

Constanze Schreiber · *In Memoriam I* · 2006
Pendant · Fine silver · 77 × 60 × 30 mm

Otto Künzli · *One Centimetre of Love* · 1996 · Pendant · Gold, polyester thread · 8 × 8 × 10 mm

Bruce Metcalf · *Heart Speaking* · 2011 · Brooch ·
Painted and gilded wood, 24k gold-plated brass · 140 x 64 mm

Iris Eichenberg → 74   Constanze Schreiber → 74   Otto Künzli → 75

ALSO IN THIS CLUSTER

189

CROWNING MOMENT

One of the most common roles played by jewellery is to mark and celebrate the milestones that measure out the course of a life. Special pieces are made and exchanged as gifts on significant occasions. **Roseanne Bartley** gently questions this practice with *One on Every Corner* by incorporating trademark emblems from McDonald's plastic spoons into a circular brooch. For those without the means to expect more from life, a shared Big Mac could be seen as qualifying as a crowning moment. **Marc Monzó's** *Big Solitaire* also suggests satire. The bigger the rock on a diamond ring the better, so this is a diamond ring blown up to the scale of a brooch. The first part of **Ben Lignel's** two-part message "I am" is only complete once it is contained within its partner "Yours" box. **Manon van Kouswijk's** necklace refers to the customary use of pearls as a gift to mark the stages in a relationship. **Karl Fritsch** crowns his silver ring with an explosion of glass stones.

Karl Fritsch · *Steinhaufen* · 2004
Ring · Silver, glass stones · 70 × 50 × 50 mm

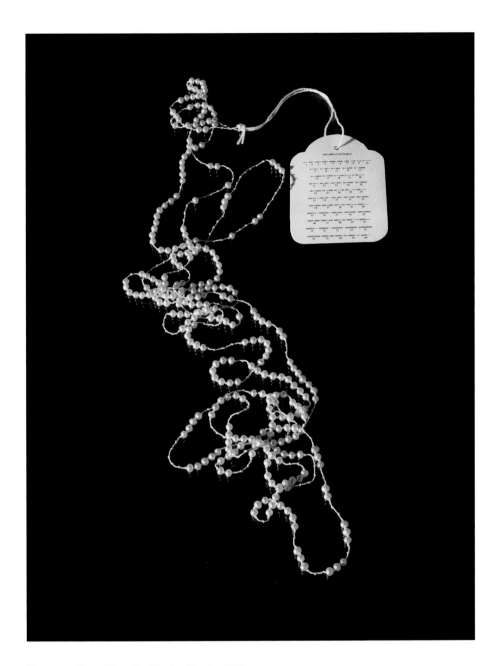

Manon van Kouswijk · *One Minute of Pearls* · 1999 ·

Necklace · Pearls, thread · Necklace: 90 mm length; Label: 50 × 50 mm

Benjamin Lignel → 76   **Marc Monzó** → 77   **Roseanne Bartley** → 77

ALSO IN THIS CLUSTER

TELL
TALES

Even if a piece of jewellery is not marking a biographical event, the jeweller can use it as a piece of narrative to tell a story, either explicitly, as is the case with **Esther Knobel's** series of brooches where she etches silver to reveal the process that has led to the creation of the object that she is embellishing or **Jamie Bennett's** delicate drawings, or more poetically, as with **Iris Nieuwenburg**, who hints at architectural spaces with her assemblage of veneer, lacquer and photographic fragments. **Herman Hermsen** also uses mysterious photographic elements, capturing images of art mixed with actual pearls. The meaning of **Jung-hoo Kim's** narrative that confronts a group of naked silver human figures with lapis lazuli raindrops is equally elusive. **Otto Künzli's** *Manhattan Piece* is a response to the trouble that a smoker has in finding public places to indulge his or her habit. It comprises a kit with a rubber tube that is hidden under clothing, connected at one end to a mouthpiece concealed within the hand and at the other end to a simple lapel adornment with a hole in its center. When the wearer draws on his or her cigarette, he or she can then direct the smoke to appear unexpectedly depending on the position of the lapel jewellery.

Jamie Bennett · *Postpriori 10 Brooch* · 2009
Brooch · Enamel, gold, copper · 60 × 65 mm

Iris Nieuwenburg · *Electroluminescente* · 2011 · Brooch · Silver, veneer, laquer, photo-print, adhesive tape · 97 × 130 × 65 mm

Jung-hoo Kim · *The Rain Drops 28* · 2010 · Brooch · .925 Silver, lapis lazuli · 93 × 88 mm

Esther Knobel → 78

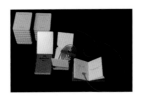

Otto Künzli → 79

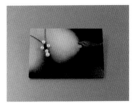

Herman Hermsen → 79

ALSO IN THIS CLUSTER

FACE VALUE

Anthropomorphic themes provide a powerful way for jewellery to communicate a message or a mood with a greater or lesser degree of literalness. **Tobias Alm's** assemblage of wood and steel graphically suggests a face with extreme economy of means, doing no more than hinting at eyes, a nose and a mouth. **Pavel Opocensky's** face brooch is reduced to almost equally basic geometric elements, but the colour and the fixed grin give it a distinctive personality. **Kim Hyewon's** brooches, on the other hand, are painfully explicit renderings of a human head in resin. **Kiko Gianocca's** rings incorporate portraits that offer different identities. **Paul Derrez** made his face as part of a project on phallic symbolism that clearly has an equally strong alternative reading to the representation of the face.

Tobias Alm · *11th Series Number 12* · 2011 · Brooch · Wood, steel · 50 × 100 × 20 mm

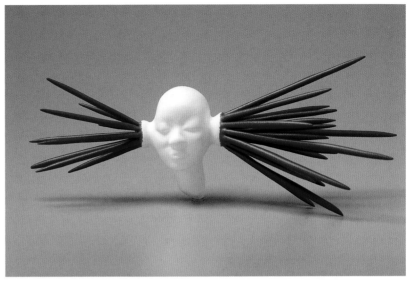

Hyewon Kim · *Remember* · 2010

Brooch · Resin, toys · 50 × 70 × 40 mm

Hyewon Kim · *Thorn 1* · 2011

Brooch · Resin, twigs · 200 × 60 × 90 mm

Kiko Gianocca → 80   Paul Derrez → 81   Pavel Opocensky → 81

ALSO IN THIS CLUSTER

MODUS OPERANDI

There are many jewellers who use their skills to ask difficult, even confrontational, questions. In this sense their work can only be understood in terms of its political meaning. None is more difficult to deal with than **Shari Pierce's** piece *36 Sexual Offenders*, which uses photographs printed on silk. It claims to portray every convicted rapist living within a five-mile radius of her workshop at the time of its making. **Benjamin Lignel** uses the form of the badge, which may or may not be understood as jewellery. The tone of his work goes from the wry—*Raise*, reversing the language of a price cut in a supermarket to mark an increase in value—to the disturbing. Printed in white on white, *Thank God I Am White* is shockingly provocative. Here, it is the message that serves to call attention to the object, a role normally played in jewellery by workmanship. *Bling Bling*, **Tjek's** stack of gold-plated brands, addresses a theme that is familiar to artists and designers from the point of view of jewellery. A more resonant message comes from **Attai Chen's** brooch. It takes the form of a bulldozer and is made from olive wood that grew on the site of a Palestinian village destroyed by Israeli settlers. **Frédéric Braham's** lotion piece refers to the practices of the cosmetic industry.

Shari Pierce · *34 Sexual Offenders and 2 Sexual Predators from Within a 5 Mile Radius* · 2011 · Necklace · Photo prints from transparencies, silk · Approx. 4,500 mm long

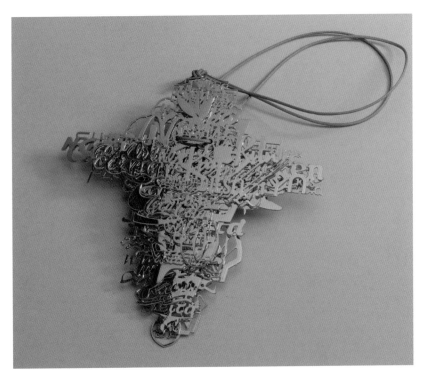

Tjek · *Bling Bling* · 2002 · Pendant · Gold-plated steel · 80 × 85 × 0.4 mm

Benjamin Lignel · *Raise* · 2011

Badge · Steel, acetate, paint, gold · 42 × 42 mm

Attai Chen → 82

Benjamin Lignel → 82

Frédéric Braham → 83

ALSO IN THIS CLUSTER

NEVER FORGET

Jewellery has an important part to play as a reminder of people and experiences and places. The contemporary form of what the Victorians called a keepsake acts as a kind of reference point in a world in which the pace of change is continually accelerating. This is not simply a question of nostalgia; it's an essential aspect of human identity and meaning. **Benjamin Lignel**, also responsible for the provocative badges shown in the *Modus Operandi* cluster, makes casts of the human ear as brooches and calls them *Thinking of You*. **Iris Eichenberg's** neck piece, with its collection of hands, traces the remnants of immigrant lives. **Monika Brugger's** medal ribbons with breasts attached were photographed by the maker as if they were military decorations pinned to the coat of an old man, who was perhaps dreaming of lost youth. **Bas Bouman's** beads could be seen as a reference to the rosary, while **Bettina Speckner's** photographic fragments recall a sense of place. **Kiko Gianocca** makes resin rectangles to be worn on the lapel; the side facing outward is blank but glossy enough for people encountering the wearer to see their own reflection. The inner face has a concealed photographic image referring to a place with significance to the wearer.

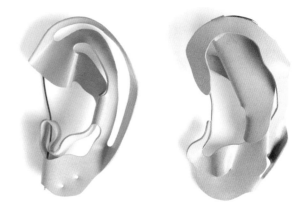

Benjamin Lignel · *Thinking of You* · 2010 · Brooches · Fine silver, industrial paint, stainless steel · 64 mm height

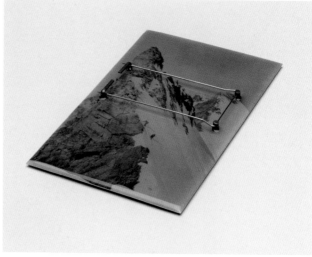

Kiko Gianocca · *Never Been There* · 2010/11 · Brooches · Silver, found image, resin · Various postcard sizes

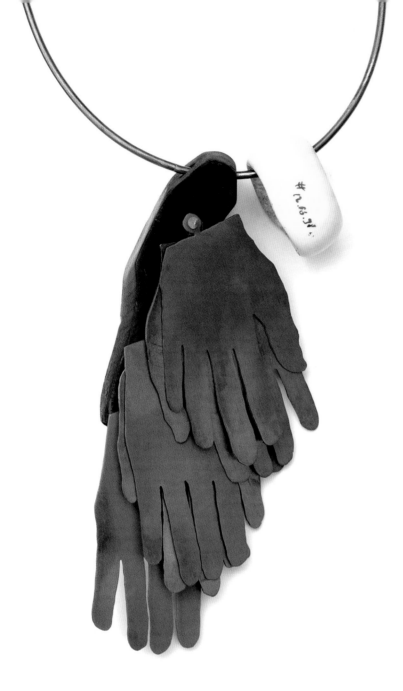

Iris Eichenberg · *Untitled* · 2007 · Neck piece ·
Silver, copper, wood, bone · 346 × 138 × 37 mm

Bettina Speckner → 84

Bas Bouman → 84

Monika Brugger → 85

ALSO IN THIS CLUSTER

EARTHLY DELIGHTS

Naturally occurring forms and finishes are an important source of inspiration for jewellers, just as they are for artists and designers. **Sam Tho Duong** has used organic materials to suggest natural phenomena; in this case, seed pearls are used to suggest ice forms. **Julie Blyfield** also uses natural objects—botanical specimens—but rather than use them to suggest other forms, she embellishes them with paint, wax and oxidised silver to maximum aesthetic effect. **Marian Hosking** explores naturally forming patterns and patinas to make complex organic jewellery. But other jewellers such as **Dongchun Lee**, **Carlier Makigawa** and **Kimiaki Kageyama** use symbolic representations of naturally occurring or organic forms to set against the clearly man-made or artificial.

Marian Hosking · *Round Boronia* · 2007
Brooch · Chemically coloured .925 silver · 90 mm diameter

Julie Blyfield · *Scintilla Series: Pink and Green Shell* · 2010
Brooches · Oxidised sterling silver, enamel paint wax · Green shell brooch: 50 × 75 × 35 mm; Seaflower: 70 × 90 × 30 mm

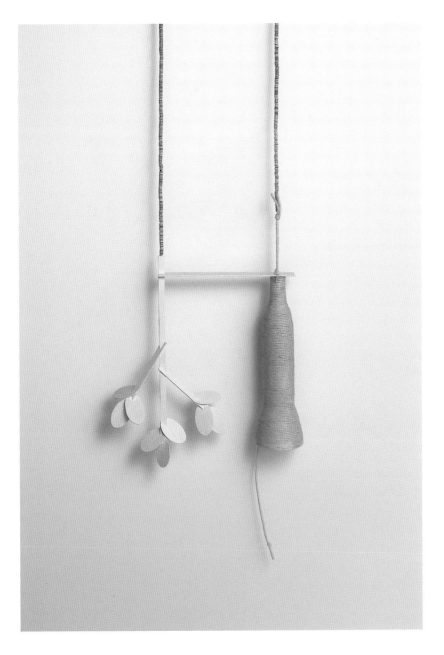

Dongchun Lee · *Inhale Exhale* · 2010

Neck piece · Pendant / thread, iron, painting · 144 × 168 × 35 mm

Kimiaki Kageyama → 86   Carlier Makigawa → 86   Sam Tho Duong → 87

ALSO IN THIS CLUSTER

ANIMAL INSTINCTS

Animals are a staple of the repertoire of imagery that jewellery can draw upon. The manner in which they are represented in aesthetic and material terms changes to reflect the current cultural interests. But the basis of the relationship with animal forms remains constant. *The Frosty Night Fox,* by **Ribbonesia**, is formed from packaging ribbon, like a particularly exquisite piece of gift wrapping. **Tom Hill's** dragonfly brooch is a contemporary version of an art-nouveau treatment of an elongated insect. **David Bielander's** *Scampi* brooch can be seen both as a piece of languidly organic curved form and a surrealist piece of Dalíesque imagery. At its most literal, jewellery has come to encompass both representations of animals and taxidermy, as exemplified in **Julia deVille's** mouse trophy. It's worth pointing out that deVille does not harm animals herself but works with creatures that have been killed accidentally. **Felieke van der Leest** creates a jokier representation of animal life, and **Alexander Blank's** duck-head trophy is a more graceful form.

Ribbonesia [Toru Yoshikawa] · *Frosty Night Fox* · 2010 ·
Brooch · Resinated ribbon · 100 × 90 × 70 mm

Tom Hill · *Dragonfly* · 2008 · Brooch · Mild steel, paint, ink · 152 × 102 mm

David Bielander · *Scampi* · 2007 · Bracelet · Silver (copper anodised), elastics · 100 mm diameter

Julia deVille → 88   Alexander Blank → 88   Felieke van der Leest → 89

ALSO IN THIS CLUSTER

TURNING POINTS

Every so often, a maker's inspiration becomes pivotal to opening up new expressions of the times and redefining what has gone before. These turning points are the markers that define the nature of the practice that follows. These works are important because they distill thinking in ways that both reflect and predict. **Otto Künzli's** bracelet *Gold Makes Blind* is one such piece. Künzli made it in response to a long-established jewellery prize, the only stipulation of which was that the winning piece must include a gold ball of a specified weight. Künzli chose to comply by making the gold entirely invisible by coating it in rubber. It was shockingly controversial at the time to question the notion of the precious, but it turned into a production piece made in substantial numbers in Künzli's workshop. **Johanna Dahm** co-opted clothing to serve as part of a jewellery piece when she used an elongated pin to skewer a garment in a carefully controlled manner. **Paul Derrez's** ring with modular interchangeable insets in a variety of materials encapsulated the modernist idea of modular design. **Esther Knobel** recycled tin to make the warrior brooches, and **Warwick Freeman's** mother-of-pearl four-pointed star focused on material qualities.

Paul Derrez · *Ring and Bracelet* · 1975/1976 · Ring and bracelet · Silver, acrylic · Various sizes

Otto Künzli · *Gold Makes Blind* · 1980 · Bangle · Rubber, gold · 77 × 78 × 12 mm

Johanna Dahm → 90

Warwick Freeman → 90

Esther Knobel → 91

ALSO IN THIS CLUSTER

HELD SECRETS

Contemporary jewellery has an everyday poetry that is amplified by the held secrets of the maker. A work will hint at something intimate and personal to be kept hidden, though as in a game, there is always an invitation to guess or solve what is not shown, even if its secret is never revealed. In the case of **Mah Rana**, the sources of the fragments that she makes are the signs of the zodiac, although they are only present tangentially. **Hans Stofer** is more enigmatic. To leave a trail of pearls across a bandage, like traces of blood or bodily fluid, can be understood in multiple ways. **Kaire Rannik's** cinder conk gift wrapped in a metal ribbon could be a trophy, a collection or a prize. **James McAllister's** pendant refers to literary texts and requires prior knowledge for the full range of meaning to become apparent. **Margaret West's** is in itself a fragment of an idea about the transience of nature. **Leonor Hipólito** subverts an industrial object to mysterious effect.

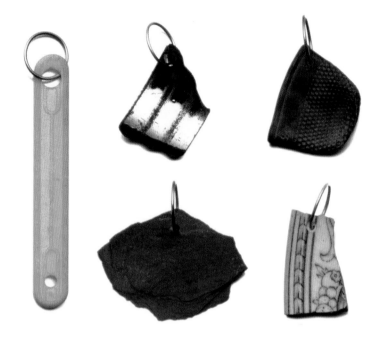

Mah Rana · *Zodiac* · 2002 · Twelve pendants · Gold, mixed media (found objects) · Gold ring 13 mm × 13 mm / various sizes

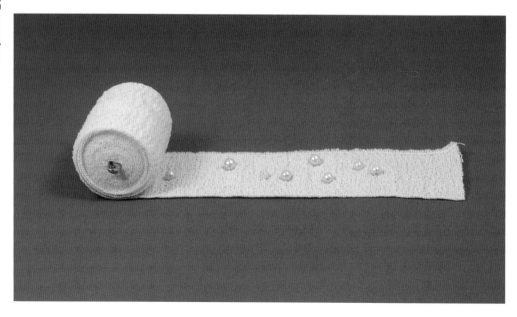

Hans Stofer · *Pearl Bracelet* · 2000 · Bracelet · Cotton, pearls, safety pin · 55 mm × 70 mm × 240 mm

Kaire Rannik · *Inonotus Obliquus* · 2010 · Brooch · Silver, copper, mirror, steel · 120 × 70 × 30 mm

James McAllister → 92   **Margaret West → 92**   **Leonor Hipólito → 93**

ALSO IN THIS CLUSTER

Origins

CHAPTER SEVEN

A Fine Line

A Fine Line offers an insight into the origins of contemporary jewellery today. Creative jewellers have always been intrigued by the essence of jewellery expressed over time, from ethnic traditions to modern status jewellery. At the same time, they have inevitably sampled or rejected ideas, approaches and technologies they have encountered in overlapping artistic disciplines as a way to find a unique creative voice.

This section features attention-grabbing pieces grouped according to their origins within diverse creative fields: inventive jewellery made by artists Alexander Calder and Anni Albers; fashion associations by Pierre Cardin and Paco Rabanne; jewellery interpretations by designers Charlotte Perriand and Ettore Sottsass; and artistic adaptations from ethnic craft traditions.

Works by key instigators of the Contemporary Jewellery Movement are presented parallel to these influencing examples. With the exception of two jewellers who are no longer alive, all these makers have continued to work in contemporary jewellery, and they are represented in other sections of the exhibition.

These origins provide a broad context for understanding the ongoing relationship between jewellery and design. Jewellery is revealed as a focal point for thinking, a point at which distinct creative fields have collided over the past sixty years. A Fine Line reminds us that the challenging spirit of contemporary jewellery can be kept alive by trading glimpses between the past and the present.

Art

The relationship between art and jewellery is long and intimate, and it hinges around the question of the physical relationship between the artist and the object. In the 1970s, Joan Sonnabend ran a gallery in New York called Sculpture to Wear. Most of what she showed took the form of limited-edition pieces. Max Ernst, Pablo Picasso and others worked with the goldsmith François Hugo to produce well-known commercial pieces. Roy Lichtenstein worked with professional enamellists to make pins, which were described by one gallery selling them as the equivalent of "three-dimensional lithographs". It is something that continues to this day. In Britain, Louisa Guinness commissioned Anish Kapoor, among others, to design pieces of jewellery. It is interesting to see the word *design* used in this context. These are all pieces that reflect an aesthetic approach but could not be seen as primary expressions. To use a term from couture fashion, this is a diffusion range for the artist.

They do not have the emotional power of works that have the physical engagement of the artist. When Hugo made a gold pendant in editions of six from a drawing by Picasso, it could never have the power of the etched portrait Picasso made on a brooch for his lover Dora Maar. And set beside the jewellery of Alexander Calder, an artist with a remarkable ability to work with his hands and to resist categorisation, limited editions look pale and insipid.

The most interesting jewellery from the art world is that which is the closest to what art used to be, and what jewellery still is. That is to say, it is art that is made by the physical intervention of the artist. But now that art has become much less concerned with the physical tactile skill of the artist and closer to an industrial process, in the manner of a Jeff Koons or a Damien Hirst, jewellery from artists who work in this way has become rather less compelling.

ABOVE · **Anni Albers** · *Necklace* · 1940 · Metal-plated drain strainer, chain and paper clips · Pendant · Drain strainer 79 mm diameter; chain: 407 mm length

OPPOSITE TOP · **Alexander Calder** · *Bird Brooch* · 1945 · Brooch · Silver and steel wire · 191 × 210 mm

OPPOSITE BOTTOM · **Alexander Calder** · *Bird Brooch* · 1945 · Brooch · Brass wire · 228.6 × 262 mm

Design

If the most powerful forms of jewellery made by artists are those with the intensity of art that reflects personal concerns and emotions, then when designers approach jewellery there are different issues at work. Charlotte Perriand used industrial materials for making jewellery as part of her explorations of modern forms of life. If you can demonstrate the potential of steel ball bearings to make necklaces, it's not hard to show that tubular steel can also make a comfortable domestic armchair.

Designers such as Ettore Sottsass had parallel practices. It would be too easy to suggest that each informed the other. He did not, as Alexander Calder did, use his own hands to make rings. He worked on such pieces as he did as a designer, by making drawings and by talking to artisan makers to understand their processes and techniques, to push them to their limits and to make objects that reflected his intentions. These were objects that reflected some of Sottsass's fascinations with the spiritual, with patterns and with colour. And these same fascinations could be seen in his other work, in his architecture and in his furniture. Perhaps more significant was its less obvious impact on his industrial work. A designer with the ability to create effective jewellery has the sensibility to understand industrial objects with a certain sophistication. You can see it in the way that Sottsass shaped the Valentine typewriter, with two vivid splashes of orange on its red body. And it is also present in his understanding of how to liberate a typewriter from the desk and turn it into a truly portable object by giving it a case that made it not only easy to carry but desirable too.

ABOVE · **Charlotte Perriand** · *Ball-bearing necklace* · 1927 ·
Necklace · Nickelled-copper · diameter: 180 mm
OPPOSITE · **Ettore Sottsass** · *Necklace* · 1967 ·
Necklace · Gold, quartz, onyx · 250 × 70 × 10 mm

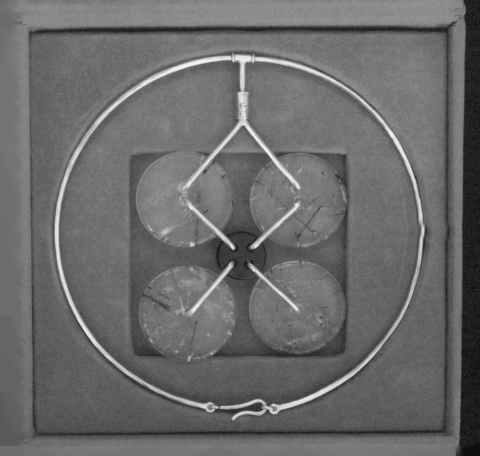

Fashion

Fashion is a phenomenon that individuals shape for themselves in the choices that they make and the uses to which they put garments and personal objects. It is also something that the individual takes on as a kind of passive consumer, dependent on the industrial-scale manufacture of imagery that fashion has become.

In the context of bags and sunglasses, as well as what are more closely identified with traditional definitions of jewellery—costume watches, earrings, bracelets and necklaces—all are extensions of fashion, as they are considered an expression of brand identity.

At its most radical level where fashion merges into the style subcultures, the appropriation of the safety pin as an item of adornment came to encapsulate an attitude toward society as much as a style or a look. It was a political signal about identity. It is hard to see a Gucci clasp or the brand on the side of a pair of dark glasses as freighted with the same level of meaning. But for all the manipulative qualities of the overheated world of contemporary fashion with huge marketing and image-creating budgets, fashion is a cultural form that has roots in design, in the craft skills of couture making and in the exploration and creation of new materials. It was textile making, after all, that led the Industrial Revolution. It consumes imagery from art and architecture, and it is skilled at the creation of imagery through photography. Jewellery, the messages about sexuality and status that it can carry and its relationship with the body are clearly an essential part of that.

ABOVE · **Pierre Cardin** · *Untitled* · 1970 ·
Neck piece/face adornment · Plastic · 180 mm width × 80 mm height
OPPOSITE · **Paco Rabanne** · *Evening Mini-Dress* · 1967
Dress · Plastic paillettes joined with metal wire

Craft

The problematic associations of the term *craft* have been endlessly rehearsed. The curator Daniel Charny brilliantly sidestepped them with his revelatory exhibition at the Victoria and Albert Museum in London in 2011, which despite being supported by the Crafts Council did not use the word *craft* in its title. He called it The Power of Making. It was a way of overcoming ultimately futile questions about the allegedly nostalgic connotations of craft. Making is as relevant to the most contemporary materials and techniques as it is to maintaining traditional skills and ways of life.

The idea of vernacular self-expression in the anthropological sense is an important root for contemporary jewellery. It is a reflection of its continuing social purpose and a reminder of the way in which it serves to measure how we define ourselves and the major events of our lives.

ABOVE · *Bella Herdsman's Pendant, Burkina Faso* · 1976 ·
Metal key rings with plastic charms · 102 mm in length ·
A Bella nomadic herdsman makes a creative decorative pendant out of the objects he finds at the local markets. The herdsmen favour bright colours and key rings with particularly eye-catching charms.

OPPOSITE · *Dinka Elder, South Sudan* · 1975 ·
Nineteenth-century Venetian chevron beads on a string of Dutch glass beads ·
The two large chevron beads are 51 mm in length ·
A Dinka elder, covered in ash, wears a rare glass bead necklace with valuable blue chevron beads from Venice and Dutch glass beads in white and pale blue. These beads would have been traded from Europe in the late nineteenth or early twentieth century.

CHAPTER EIGHT

A Brief Contemporary Jewellery History

Susan Cohn

As a dedicated group of loosely aligned
makers, contemporary jewellery has
experienced enough to have a history.
What contemporary jewellery is and
where it comes from is never entirely clear.
It sits within a long tradition of jewellery
and gained momentum in an age where
artistic movements mattered. Today,
questions of history are usually troubling.
As movements age they look to the past,
sometimes with nostalgia, and this is
not a bad thing, for looking at a movement
as a past can instigate fresh thinking,
new work and unknown trajectories.

By the time his book, *Contemporary Jewellery, A Critical Assessment 1945–1975* went into print in 1976, Ralph Turner was writing against a background in which the exchange between contemporary art and jewellery had been clearly discernable for some time, in the experimentations of the Bauhaus and in the activities of some highly visible artists, not least—Picasso, Dalí and the Pomodoro brothers in Europe, Calder in America.[1] Progressive jewellers—though less visible (they appear to have gained less exposure than these artists)—were also starting to experiment with radical jewellery expressions.

Peter Dormer writes in *Jewellery of Our Time* that contemporary jewellery has developed "in dialogue with modernism."[2] Historically, the Contemporary Jewellery Movement was instigated in a period when major art movements (pop art, op art, constructivism) were engaged in a broad cultural reappraisal of modernism. The strong impetus in art schools was toward challenging "mainstream" traditions of seeing the art-object. Glenn Adamson, in his contribution to this book, makes a compelling point that contemporary jewellers appear to have aligned with the surrealists in embracing an "alternative commercialism" that blends high art

→ 96

and mass culture. From a maker's perspective, the mutual attraction between surrealism and contemporary jewellery might seem obvious: jewellery has a unique vocabulary well suited to the aims of artists concerned with adapting the language of inner life to the world of our possessions. And, as Dormer notes, surrealism has proven "continuously attractive to artists who want to explore the human-made world in terms of its values and the emotions it stimulates in us."[3] It is reasonable to suggest that through its influence on art and popular culture, surrealism opened the door for a plurality of narratives to enter jewellery discourse.

There was a key point of difference between the art movements and the Contemporary Jewellery Movement. The latter operated in the shadow of an established jewellery industry with strong national traditions and commercial presence. Throughout the 1960s, jewellery continued in popular imagination to be considered a luxury item that derives value through the use of precious materials—in fact, the seductions of a highly visible, expensive display continue to underline jewellery's commercial trade today. These expectations provided a unique framework for cultural resistance.

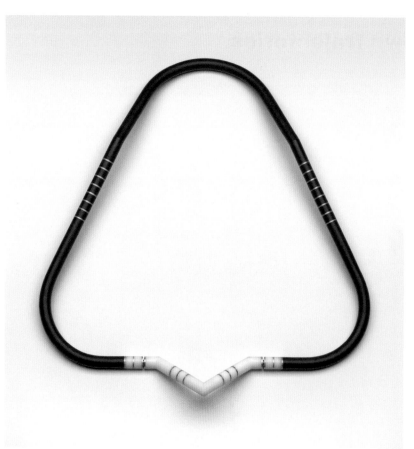

LEFT · **David Watkins** · *Triangular Neckpiece* · 1976 · Neck piece · Coloured synthetic polymer resin, gold · 294 × 268 × 29 mm
OPPOSITE · **Wendy Ramshaw** · *Necklace Without Direction* · 1977 · Necklace · 750 gold, enamel · 272 × 138 × 9 mm

Intense experimentation was led by aesthetic considerations over ideological concerns. This changed in the 1970s. Makers became influenced by debates and movements across art, craft and design, and were impacted by the rise of new consumer and media cultures. Together, they sought to make jewellery democratic and renew its connection to the body, to question jewellery's social role and to experiment with new materials. These concerns provided the intellectual axes along which new jewellers began to connect, align and speak out with coherent voice.

Exchange of ideas and techniques benefited from proactive networking on an increasingly international scale. Through conferences, competitions, publications and an extensive programme of international public events, leaders in the field began to distinguish themselves. Hermann Jünger, an inventive artist and an influential teacher, established jewellery making as an autonomous creative discipline at the Academie der Bildenden Künste in Munich. He taught many jewellers and promoted strong, experimental thinking through his exhibitions and writings.[4] New art schools were still being built—a residue from postwar reconstruction efforts—and key figures from the new movement were invited to teach in them. Claus Bury led activities in England, Israel, America and Australia. His experimentation in metal alloys and acrylics had a profound impact, engendering a new aesthetic that evoked pop-art imagery.

German, Dutch, American and British makers already had established traditions in jewellery craftsmanship, style, narrative and artistic experimentation on which to draw in developing their own distinctive national voices. These countries became the centres to an international movement. Their governments set up special bodies such as the Crafts Council of Great Britain, the Society of North American Goldsmiths and the Crafts Council of Australia. Major public art galleries and museums promoted new work, with jewellery collections developed and special exhibitions held by Stedelijk in Amsterdam, The Museum of Modern Art in New York and the National Gallery of Victoria in Melbourne, among others. Australian jewellers, like others removed from the European circumstance, were less radical or purposeful in crafting a national voice through new jewellery styles.

LEFT · **Robert Smit** · *Brooch* · 1986 ·
Brooch · 1000 gold, 750 gold
OPPOSITE · **Gijs Bakker** · *Shoulder Piece* · 1967 ·
Shoulder piece · Anodised aluminium · 200 × 206 × 204 mm

Through the 1970s contemporary jewellery benefited from a problem-solving approach that came out of modernist art and design principles. From the early 1960s, makers had responded to modernism's design aesthetic—the use of industrial materials, clean simple lines, an absence of decorative detailing apart from elements like rivets or screws. The problem-solving approach can be attributed as having grown out of the Dutch De Stijl movement.[5] Gijs Bakker and Emmy van Leersum developed a strategy for emphasising jewellery ideas through design, exploiting industrial materials (textiles, rubber, aluminium) and high craft with a minimum of making.[6] The Dutch jewellers used nonprecious materials and design principles to encourage audiences as well as other makers to engage with ideas and content above other allures.

Design approaches helped jewellers assume intellectual control in working new style. With greater autonomy in the process from conception to manufacture, they could further test the boundaries to expectations—Bakker and van Leersum, for instance, extended their approach into experimental clothing. Contemporary jewellers sought to draw attention back to the body through techniques of abstraction, treating the body as a background for jewellery's invention and display.

The 1980s were the Contemporary Jewellery Movement's "golden years". The public and private debates central to the movement were tuned in response to a new postmodern age.[7] The processes of globalisation had accelerated, underscored by changing economic conditions and rapid invention of new technologies, products and communications. The Walkman, launched in 1979, became symbolic of an age obsessed with appearances and customisation, private pleasures and public display. In the street displays of spectacular subcultures, as on television screens in private living rooms, the new meaning of style was painted thick. Objects were produced, adapted, bought, owned and worn to encode new forms of taste, identity and group belonging.

ABOVE · **Otto Künzli** · *Wallpaper Brooches* · 1982 · Brooch · Wallpaper, synthetic polymer core, steel · Various sizes

OPPOSITE · **Hermann Jünger** · *Choker with Fourteen Interchangeable Pendants* · 1978/1979 · Neck piece · Gold, silver, gilt-metal, crystal, enamel, jasper, ivory, tombac · Various sizes

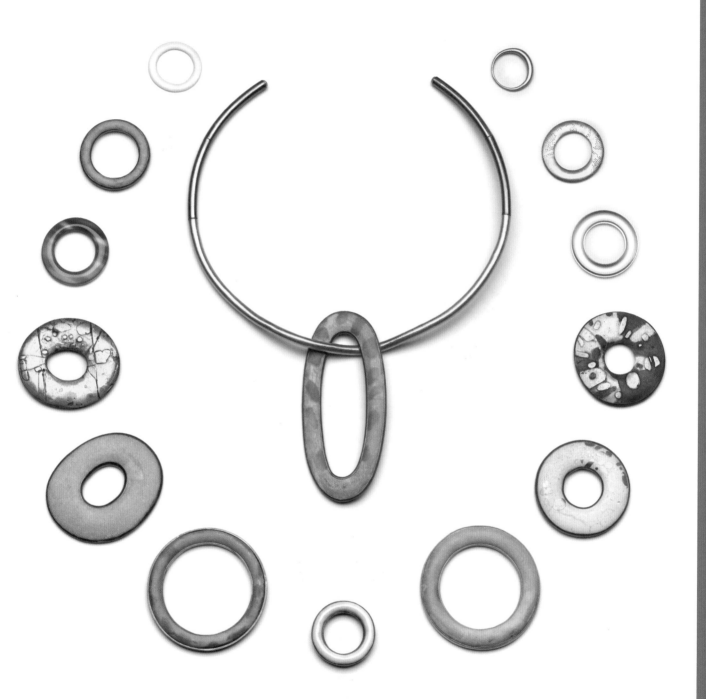

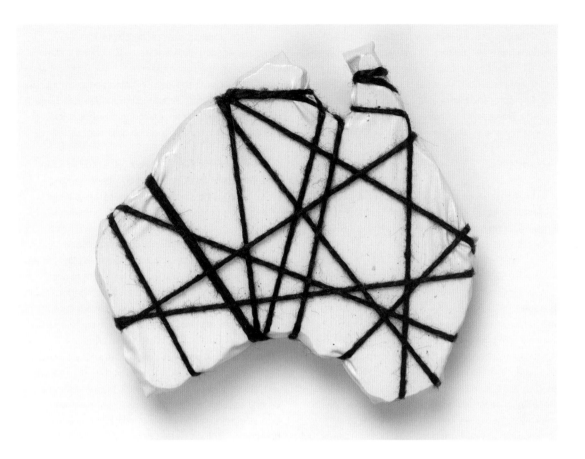

Debates over future directions for practice began to polarise the field. How, jewellers debated, should the movement respond in liberating jewellery's intrinsic values while pushing the limits to its invention and performance? The most contentious debate—and root to all others—was on the "proper" function of jewellery. Views diverged on matters of materials (precious or nonprecious), wearability (jewellery or sculpture) and value (elite or democratic). Makers sought to differentiate themselves on a number of grounds: artistic focus (biographical or political), positioning (art or craft) and intended audience (gallery or shop).

Many makers were hooked on the agenda at the heart of the movement. They aimed to make jewellery experimental, democratic and nonprecious, and vocally rejected using any type of precious materials. At the decade's beginning, this approach was shadowed by slumping financial conditions bringing hugely inflated prices for gold. By mid-decade, the debate had gained significant momentum. Some reacted against the use of cheap materials, asserting that this led to superficial work. Too much emphasis on materials, they contended, led jewellers to forgo skill, sacrifice idea and demolish jewellery's natural aura.

The debate played out to its fullest extent in Holland, where public exchanges between Gijs Bakker and Robert Smit gave fierce articulation to the opposing positions and contributed to a crystallisation of the field. In her essay in this book, Liesbeth den Besten takes → 102 Bakker's and Smit's exchange to stand for a broader problem faced by contemporary jewellers: the influence of modernism was to sever the connection between art and beauty, but jewellers have long sought inspiration in the dynamics between beauty, preciousness and workmanship. While design could function (even flourish) through a period of aesthetic deconstruction, contemporary jewellers consciously sought strategies to rethink beauty through making. So, Liesbeth writes, "in the course of the decade, the idea of finding aesthetic quality, beauty, in imperfection rather than perfection, gradually replaced the aesthetic of modernism".

OPPOSITE · **Peter Tully** · *Love Me Tender* · 1977 · Necklace · Plastic, paste, opaque synthetic polymer resin, mirror, colour-offset lithograph, enamel paint · 384 × 140 × 14 mm

ABOVE · **Peter Tully** · *Christo Australia* · 1982 · Brooch · Transparent synthetic polymer resin, plastic, cotton thread, steel · 53 × 56 × 12 mm

Bakker would eventually return to the use of precious materials, putting his past attitudes in historical context. "Society and politics change and the world is a different place now", he would reflect. "When Emmy [van Leersum] and I were young there was far less equality. Nowadays most of us are more or less equal—at least in Holland." Bakker went on to highlight the relationship between jewellery and culture as a two-way street.

> "The message we gave out with our radical forms and new materials was done with conviction almost thirty years ago: it made its impact then and so we moved on with society."[8]

The 1960s had celebrated youth; in the 1970s the cult of the body had emerged; and by the 1980s "body beautiful" culture was in full swing.[9] While diversity in jewellery expression reigned, experimentation with adorning the body took new directions. Making practice was opened into novel artistic spaces—claimed as sculpture, installed in galleries and presented as performance, stimulating new conversations. Pierre Degen applied interpretive art processes to deconstruct the limits of jewellery and its relation to the body. Degen created visually striking jewellery structures to be worn or carried, utilising everyday objects like ladders alongside objects he invented.[10] Art jewellery not only stretched the boundaries of jewellery, it encouraged art makers and collectors to engage with the field. This opened contemporary jewellery to a charge that, through its practice, makers were reverting back to a new elitism.

The mid-1980s saw another generation come to the fore. Young makers, trained through university courses in traditions of hand making, tended to situate their practices in studio production. Dormer observes that soft precision, a signature of most studio production, owes much to German jewellery aesthetics and the approach of making through design.[11] But a range of factors brought this style to international prominence. Jewellers facing the economic pressures of working for themselves had to embrace simplicity in their practice. Beyond this rationale, many jewellers rejected the vision of mass machine–directed manufacture idealised in modernist art and design. They associated with the craft movement in valuing workmanship and making traditions. The emotional and intellectual experience of making was seen to lie in the exploration of formal aesthetics via hand-tool processes.

Nonetheless, new technologies and new materials enabled different ways of working and many makers developed an interest in semi-mass-produced work, playing with the idea as motivation and materials as the means. Some extended the modernist approach into postmodern terrain, exploring tensions between the unique and multiple through both exhibition and production work.

By the mid-1980s makers were producing an international style of ideas and jewellery themes. Dormer suggests that these are loosely organised into three subcategories, each accommodating a range of expression.[12] Makers working toward an abstract style focused mainly on materials and design. Jewellers working in the figurative style explored image and narrative. And radical jewellers sought to push jewellery's boundaries into sculpture and performance. Consolidation of styles empowered makers to form their own artistic identities—sometimes in resistance to trends within the field. Otto Künzli critiques contemporary jewellery through its invention, crossing all three styles. Künzli introduced portrait photography as a device to project critical voice. In a photographic series, his large wallpaper brooches are modelled on the bodies of middle-class professionals. Image and object combined highlight contemporary jewellery's use as a status symbol and the field's narrow audience focus. For Künzli, this reflective wit, transposed into jewellery style, has become emblematic of his critical position and artistic identity.

For makers working in an age obsessed with images, the photograph contrived to illustrate "real" people wearing "real" jewellery. But it also became a key device for makers to project their own voices as authors. Throughout the 1980s there was a general orientation toward jewellery as "signature"—a term both Turner and Dormer use in their histories of the period.[13] Questions regarding authorship and authenticity were brought to the fore. This reflected the increasing impact of postmodern thinking over art makers, critics and audiences.[14] Within contemporary jewellery circles, new jewellery had in effect been translated into a form of subcultural capital, with makers sampling widely from popular culture, fashion and street appearance.

The channel of engagement was not one-way—the works of Caroline Broadhead (a jeweller) and Issey Miyake (a fashion designer) illustrate the mutual feeding of ideas that took place. But while this crossover does suggest that contemporary jewellery engaged beyond its own boundaries, it is equally likely that these sampling practices were a case of the field "stage managing" itself (to use Dormer's words). That is, jewellers were assembling a kind of cultural currency that would inform internally directed displays of authentic belonging.

The 1980s were a radical period for invention, performances and debates in contemporary jewellery. Makers experimented with wearers and bodies, while testing the boundaries of jewellery as an object and practice. By the 1990s, signature had been invented and repetition settled in. For some, the Contemporary Jewellery Movement had not just reached its zenith but come to a decisive end—even as contemporary jewellery continues unabated as an inventive practice. For jewellers and audiences equally, in evaluating work, increasing emphasis has been placed on authentic stories in craft and "star" status of the maker, over renewed questioning about jewellery values. Potentially, this is the outcome from an inherent push and pull between art and design, which new jewellers—more than ever—must negotiate in a deliberate manner if their work is to remain relevant through periods of profound global transition.

Mah Rana · *Jewellery is Life* · 2001 · Badge · Steel, paper · 25 × 25 mm

Contributors

KEY

RP: REPRESENTED BY

TG: TEACHING POSITIONS

WR: WRITER

HELEN AITKEN-KUHNEN → 166

Queanbeyan, NSW, Australia

Codirector of Workshop Bilk, Queanbeyan, NSW, Australia · www.workshopbilk.com

FRAN ALLISON → 66

Auckland, New Zealand

TG: Senior Lecturer at Manukau School of Visual Arts, Auckland, New Zealand · fran.allison@manukau.ac.nz

TOBIAS ALM → 194

Stockholm, Sweden

RP: Galerie Platina · Galerie Rob Koudijs · www.tobiasalm.com

RON ARAD → 176

London, United Kingdom

Ron Arad Associates, London, UK · **RP:** Chi ha paura…? · www.ronarad.com

ROBERT BAINES → 169

Melbourne, VIC, Australia

TG: Professor of Art, Gold and Silversmithing, School of Art, RMIT University, Melbourne, VIC, Australia · **RP:** Galerie Biró · Galerie Marzee · robert.baines@rmit.edu.au

GIJS BAKKER → 56, 62, 63, 108, 109, 134, 153, 178, 225

Amsterdam, The Netherlands

Gijs Bakker Design, Amsterdam, The Netherlands · Creative Director, Chi ha paura…? The Netherlands · Creative Director, Yii, Taiwan · Advisor, American Craft Museum, New York, New York, USA · **TG:** Head of Masters Course, Design Academy, Eindhoven, The Netherlands · **RP:** Galerie Ra · Galery Stühler · Galerie Sofie Lachaert · Gallery Helen Drutt · Marijke Studio · Gallery Deux Poissons · www.gijsbakker.com · www.chihapaura.com

RUT-MALIN BARKLUND → 165

Stockholm, Sweden

RP: Galerie Platina · www.rut-malin.se

ROSEANNE BARTLEY → 77

Melbourne, VIC, Australia

RP: Charon Kransen Arts · bartleybila@gmail.com

NICHOLAS BASTIN → 172

Melbourne, VIC, Australia

TG: Lecturer, School of Art, RMIT University, Melbourne, VIC, Australia · **RP:** Charon Kransen Arts · www.nicholasbastin.com

JAMIE BENNETT → 192

Stone Ridge, New York, United States

TG: Professor of Art, School of Fine & Performing Arts, State University of New York, New Paltz, New York, USA · bennettj@newpaltz.edu

DAVID BIELANDER → 203

Munich, Germany

(with Helen Britton and Yutaka Minegishi)

RP: Galerie Biró · Galerie Beatrice Lang, Galerie Rob Koudijs · Gallery Funaki · Galerie SO · Ornamentum Gallery · Jewelers'werk Galerie · Klimt02 Gallery · davidbielander@mac.com

ALEXANDER BLANK → 69, 88

Munich, Germany

RP: Galerie Rob Koudijs · alex.blank@web.de

BLESS [INES KAAG AND DESIRÉE HEISS] → 178

Paris, France, and Berlin, Germany

RP: Chi ha paura…? · www.bless-service.de

JULIE BLYFIELD → 200

Adelaide, SA, Australia

RP: Gallery Funaki · Galerie Ra · Charon Kransen Arts · jblyfield@adam.com.au

BAS BOUMAN → 84

Haarlem, The Netherlands

RP: Galerie Louise Smit · basbouman76@hotmail.com

FRÉDÉRIC BRAHAM → 83

Antibes, France

RP: Galerie Biró · Charon Kransen Arts · frederic.braham@free.fr

HELEN BRITTON → 44

Munich, Germany (with David Bielander and Yutaka Minegishi)

RP: Galerie Louise Smit · Galerie Sofie Lachaert · Gallery Funaki · Gallery Beatrice Lang · Gallery Hélène Poree · Gallery Pilartz · helenbritton@mac.com

CAROLINE BROADHEAD → 65

London, United Kingdom

TG: Course Director, BA Jewellery, Central Saint Martins, University of the Arts, London, UK · **RP:** Marsden Woo Gallery · c.broadhead@csm.arts.ac.uk

MAISIE BROADHEAD → 138, 139

London, United Kingdom

RP: Sarah Myerscough Gallery, London, UK · Sienna Gallery, Lenox, Massachusetts, USA · www.maisiebroadhead.com

SIGURD BRONGER → 184

Oslo, Norway

RP: Galerie Ra · www.sigurdbronger.no

MONIKA BRUGGER → 85, 118, 119

Paimpont, France

TG: Professor, Jewellery studio, ENSA (Ecole national superière d'art) Limoges-Aubusson, France · Teacher, History of Contemporary Jewellery, AFEDAP (Association pour la formation et le développement des arts plastiques), Paris, France · **RP:** Galerie Pilartz · Alternatives Gallery · Galerie Noel Guyomarc'h · monkbrugger@free.fr

DOUG BUCCI → 177

Philadelphia, Pennsylvania, United States

TG: Part-time Assistant Professor, Industrial Design, University of the Arts, Philadelphia, Pennsylvania, USA · Part-time Assistant Professor, Metals/Jewelry/CAD-CAM, Tyler School of Art, Philadelphia, Pennsylvania, USA · www.dougbucci.com

PETER CHANG → 187

Glasgow, Scotland, United Kingdom

www.peterchang.org

ATTAI CHEN → 82

Munich, Germany

RP: Galerie Spektrum · Gallery Loupe · attaichen@gmail.com

NORMAN CHERRY → 149,

Lincoln, United Kingdom

TG: Dean of Faculty, Lincoln School of Art and Design, University of Lincoln, Lincoln, UK · **RP:** Alternatives Gallery · ncherry@lincoln.ac.uk

LIN CHEUNG → 179

London, United Kingdom

TG: Senior Lecturer, BA (Hons) Jewellery Design, Central Saint Martins College of Art & Design, London, UK · Visiting Lecturer, BA (Hons) Jewellery & Silversmithing, Edinburgh College of Art, · University of Edinburgh, UK · Visiting Lecturer, BA (Hons) Jewellery, Middlesex University, UK · **RP:** Gallery Deux Poissons · Chi ha paura…? · www.lincheung.co.uk

SIMON COTTRELL → 162

Melbourne, VIC, Australia

TG: Associate Lecturer, Fine Arts, Monash University, Melbourne, VIC, Australia · **RP:** Gallery Funaki · Charon Kransen Arts · simon.cottrell@hotmail.com

JOHANNA DAHM → 90, 160

Zürich and Intragna, Switzerland

TG: Tenured Professor at Pforzheim University, Dept. of Jewellery and Everyday Objects, Germany · **RP:** Galerie Ra · Ornamentum Gallery · dahmjohanna@gmx.ch

PAUL DERREZ → 81, 130, 204

Amsterdam, The Netherlands

Director, Galerie Ra, Amsterdam, The Netherlands · **RP:** Galerie Ra · Gallery Funaki · Galerie Biró · www.galerie-ra.nl

JULIA DEVILLE → 88

Melbourne, VIC, Australia

RP: Sophie Gannon Gallery · www.discemori.com

GEORG DOBLER → 48

Berlin, Germany

TG: Professor, Metal Design, Design Faculty, HAWK (Hochschule für Angewandte Wissenschaft und Kunst), Hildesheim, Germany · **RP:** Gallerie Spectrum · dobler@hawk-hhg.de

SAM THO DUONG → 87

Pforzheim, Germany

RP: Galerie Ra · Ornamentum Gallery · www.gogotho.de

MARK EDGOOSE → 51

Melbourne, VIC, Australia

TG: Senior Lecturer, Coordinator, Undergraduate Gold and Silversmithing, School of Art, RMIT University, Melbourne, VIC, Australia · mark.edgoose@rmit.edu.au

IRIS EICHENBERG → 74, 199

Bloomfield Hills, Michigan, United States

TG: Head of Metalsmithing, Cranbrook Academy of Art, Bloomfield Hills, Michigan, USA · **RP:** Galerie Louise Smit · Gallery Ornamentum · Galerie SO · Gallery Platina · Galerie Verzameld Werk · Galerie Spektrum · Gallery Deux Poissons · Paul Kotula Projects · www.iriseichenberg.nl

WARWICK FREEMAN

→ 45, 50, 90

Auckland, New Zealand

RP: Galerie Ra · Gallery Funaki · Gallery Deux Poissons · Fingers Jewellery · starform@xtra.co.nz

KARL FRITSCH → 55, 190

Wellington, New Zealand

RP: Galerie Ra · Jewellers'werk Gallery · Gallery Funaki · Galeria Hipotesi · Fingers Gallery · StudioGR 20 · Galerie Viceversa · Gallery Deux Poissons · Galerie Sofie Lachaert · Galerie Biró · Galerie Reverso · schmuckfritsch@mac.com

MARI FUNAKI (1950–2010)

→ 180, 181

Melbourne, VIC, Australia

Director (1994–2010), Gallery Funaki · gallery@galleryfunaki.com.au

SUSIE GANCH → 43

Richmond, Virginia, United States

TG: Assistant Professor, Head of Craft / Material Studies, School of the Arts, Virginia Commonwealth University, Richmond, Virginia, USA · Codirector Radical Jewelery Makeover · **RP:** Velvet da Vinci · Sienna Gallery · Quirk Gallery · www.susieganch.com

KIKO GIANOCCA → 80, 198

Origlio, Switzerland

RP: Galerie Ra · Galerie Wittenbrink · Verzameld Werk · Maurer Zilioli Contemporary Arts · Gallery Funaki · kikogianocca@bluewin.ch

CHRISTINE GRAF → 164

Munich, Germany

RP: Galerie Ra · cg.christine.graf@web.de

ANDY GUT → 141, 172

Pforzheim, Germany

TG: Professor for Jewellery School of Design, Pforzheim University, Pforzheim, Germany · **RP:** Galerie SO · Jewelers'werk Galerie · andy.gut@hs-pforzheim.de

URSULA GUTTMANN → 152

Linz, Austria

RP: Gallery Hélène Poree · www.ursulaguttmann.com

HERMAN HERMSEN → 79

Oosterbeek, The Netherlands

TG: University of Applied Science, Düsseldorf, Germany · **RP:** Galerie Ra · Gallery Deux Poissons · Galerie Marzee · hermanhermsen@planet.nl

THERESE HILBERT → 132, 144, 170

Munich, Germany

RP: Galerie Ra · Gallery Funaki · theresehilbert@yahoo.de

TOM HILL → 202

San Francisco, California, United States

RP: Velvet da Vinci · wiretom@earthlink.net

LEONOR HIPÓLITO → 93

Lisbon, Portugal

RP: Galerie Reverso · Gallery Deux Poissons · www.leonorhipolito.com

GABRIELA HORVAT → 47

Buenos Aires, Argentina

www.gabrielahorvat.com

MARIAN HOSKING → 41, 200

Melbourne, VIC, Australia

TG: Department of Fine Art, Monash University, Melbourne, VIC, Australia · **RP:** Gallery Funaki · Galerie Ra · Workshop Bilk · marian.hosking@monash.ed

JOHN IVERSEN → 44

East Hampton, New York, United States

RP: Ornamentum Gallery · Jewelers'werk Galerie · johniversen@verizon.net

JUNGJUNG ITOMIKA → 167

Tokyo, Japan

RP: Gallery Deux Poissons · www.jungjung.jp

YONG-IL JEON → 170

Seoul, South Korea

TG: Professor, Metalwork & Jewellery Department, Kookmin University, Seoul, South Korea · jeon@kookmin.ac.kr

SVENJA JOHN → 56

Berlin, Germany

RP: Gallery Funaki · Galerie Ra · Galerie Biró · Gallery Deux Poissons · Galerie Aurum, Frankfurt, Germany · Jewelers'werk Galerie · www.svenja-john.de

HERMANN JÜNGER (1928–2005)

→ 226

Zorneding, Germany

TG: Head (1972–1990), Goldsmith, Akademie der Bildenden Künste, Munich, Germany

KIMIAKI KAGEYAMA → 86

Uenohara-shi, Yamanashi-ken, Japan

TG: Professor, Jewellery, Hiko Mizuno Jewellery College, Tokyo, Japan · **RP:** Gallery Deux Poissons · Galerie SO · kageyama@jewelry.ac.jp · kimiaki.kageyama@nifty.com

JIRO KAMATA → 43

Munich, Germany

TG: Assistant Professor, Jewellery Department, Akademie der Bildenden Künste, Munich, Germany · **RP:** Gallery Deux Poissons · Gallery Funaki · Galerie Rob Koudijs · Ornamentum Gallery · Klimt02 Gallery · www.jirokamata.com

BEPPE KESSLER → 50

Amsterdam, The Netherlands

RP: Galerie Louise Smit · Galerie Hélène Poree · Gallery Aurum · Galerie V & V · Galerie Annick Zufferey · www.beppekessler.nl

HYEWON KIM → 195

Seoul, South Korea

kimhyewon80@naver.com

JUNG-HOO KIM → 193

Seoul, South Korea

junghookim@yahoo.co.kr

SUSANNE KLEMM → 120

Amsterdam, The Netherlands

RP: Galerie Annick Zufferey · Gallery Deux Poissons · Galerie Ra · Galerie Jungblut · Galerie Friends of Carlotta · www.susanneklemm.com

ESTHER KNOBEL → 41, 78, 91

Jerusalem, Israel

RP: Galerie Ra · Jewelers'werk Galerie · stknobel@netvision.net.il

DANIEL KRUGER → 168

Berlin, Germany

TG: Professor, Jewellery, Burg Giebichenstein · University of Art and Design, Halle (Saale), Germany · **RP:** Gallery Funaki · Galerie Slavik · Galerie Ra · Sienna Gallery · Galerie Biró · Gallery Sofie Lachaert · kruger@burg-halle.de

JOHANNES KUHNEN → 171

Queanbeyan, NSW, Australia

Jeweller and Codirector of Workshop Bilk Canberra, ACT, Australia · **TG:** Associate Professor, Gold and Silversmithing, School of Art, Australian National University, Canberra, ACT, Australia · www.workshopbilk.com

OTTO KÜNZLI → 75, 79, 154, 155, 188, 205

Munich, Germany

TG: Professor, Jewellery Department, Akademie der Bildenden Künste, Munich, Germany · Visiting Professor, Royal College of Art, London, UK · **RP:** Gallery Funaki · Galerie Wittenbrink · Galerie SO · Galerie Marzee · Gallery Deux Poissons · ottokuenzli@yahoo.de

FLORIAN LADSTÄTTER → 127

Vienna, Austria

www.florian-design.com

SIMONE LEAMON → 178

Melbourne, VIC, Australia

WR: Editor-at-large, *How We Create* · Columnist, *Indesign* Australia · www.howwecreate.com.au · www.indesignmag.com · www.simoneleamon.com

DONGCHUN LEE → 201

Seoul, South Korea

TG: Associate Professor, Metalwork & Jewelry Department, College of Design, Kookmin University, Seoul, South Korea · **RP:** Galerie Marzee · jewelee@kookmin.ac.kr

BENJAMIN LIGNEL
→ 76, 82, 197, 198

Paris, France

RP: Alternatives Gallery · Velvet da Vinci · Flow Gallery · Lesley Craze Gallery · Klimt02 Gallery · www.benjaminlignel.com

SARI LIIMATTA → 122

Lappeenranta, Finland

RP: Galerie Rob Koudijs · Klimt02 Gallery · www.sariliimatta.net

NEL LINSSEN → 46, 166

Nijmegen, The Netherlands

RP: Gallery Funaki · Charon Kransen Arts · Galerie Slavik · Gallery Sofie Lachaert · Galerie Hilde Leiss · Galerie Viceversa · Galerie Ra · Galerie Marzee · The Scottish Gallery · www.nellinssen.nl

SUE LORRAINE → 40

Adelaide, SA, Australia

TG: Arts Development Officer, Public Art & Design Unit, Arts SA, Government of South Australia · Partner, Gray Street Workshop, Adelaide, SA, Australia · **RP:** Gallery Funaki · www.graystreetworkshop.com.au

SUSKA MACKERT → 150, 151

Amsterdam, The Netherlands / Hamburg, Germany

TG: Head of Jewellery Department, Gerrit Rietveld Academie, Amsterdam, The Netherlands · **RP:** Galerie Rob Koudijs · Galerie Spektrum · www.suskamackert .com · suska@suskamackert.com

FRITZ MAIERHOFER → 49

Vienna, Austria

RP: Caroline Van Hoek Gallery · Klimt02 Gallery · www.fritz-maierhofer.com ·

CARLIER MAKIGAWA → 86, 144

Melbourne, VIC, Australia

RP: Gallery Funaki · Workshop Bilk · carlier@bigpond.net.au

MIA MALJOJOKI → 173

Munich, Germany

RP: Galerie Rob Koudijs · Galerie Spektrum · Galerie Noel Guyomarc'h · www.miamaljojoki.com

SALLY MARSLAND → 41, 55

Melbourne, VIC, Australia

RP: Gallery Funaki · Galerie SO · sal_marsland@hotmail.com

JAMES MCALLISTER → 92

Melbourne, VIC, Australia

phenotype14@optusnet.com.au

BRUCE METCALF → 189

Bala Cynwyd, Pennsylvania, United States

RP: Sienna Gallery · Snyderman Works Galleries · www.brucemetcalf.com

YUTAKA MINEGISHI → 45

Munich, Germany

RP: Gallery Funaki · Galerie Louise Smit · www.yutakaminegishi.com

TAWEESAK MOLSAWAT → 54

Bangkok, Thailand

TG: Instructor, Industrial Design (Jewelry & Metalsmithing), King Mongkut's Institute of Technology, Ladkrabang, Bangkok, Thailand · **RP:** Sculpture to Wear · tmolsawat@hotmail.com

MARC MONZÓ → 77, 158

Barcelona, Spain

RP: Gallery Funaki · Four · Gallery Sofie Lachaert · Oona Galerie · Galerie Wittenbrink · Galerie Louise Smit · Galerie Reverso · Galerie SO · Pedras e Pessegosl · Klimt02 Gallery · Vallery · Ornamentum Gallery · Galerie Noel Guyomarc'h · Gallery Deux Poissons · www.marcmonzo.net

KAZUMI NAGANO → 164

Tokyo, Japan

RP: Galerie Pilartz · Galerie Slavik · knagano@hf.catv.ne.jp

SHUNICHIRO NAKASHIMA → 161

Kanazawa, Japan

TG: Assistant Professor, Department of Craft (Weaving), Kanazawa College of Art, Kanazawa, Ishikawa, Japan · **RP:** Gallery Deux Poissons · nakashima@kanazawa-bidai.ac.jp

IRIS NIEUWENBURG → 192

Rotterdam, The Netherlands

RP: Galerie Louise Smit · Droog Design · irisnieuwenburg@hotmail.com

TED NOTEN → 38, 58, 59, 183

Amsterdam, The Netherlands

RP: Galerie Rob Koudijs · Galerie SO · Klimt02 Gallery · Gallery Deux Poissons · Ornamentum Gallery · www.tednoten.com

PAVEL OPOCENSKY → 81

Prague, Czech Republic

RP: Galerie Ra · Galerie Marzee · Galerie Slavik · Galerie Biró · pavel.opocensky@centrum.cz

TIFFANY PARBS → 67, 148

Melbourne, VIC, Australia

tiffparbs@iinet.net.au

NOON PASSAMA → 53

Amsterdam, The Netherlands

RP: Galerie Ra · Galerie Wittenbrink · Oona Galerie · Atta Gallery · www.noonpassama.com

ADAM PAXON → 52

Keswick, Cumbria, United Kingdom

adampaxon@yahoo.co.uk

RUUDT PETERS → 49

Amsterdam and Ravenstein, The Netherlands

TG: Professor, Alchimia Contemporary Jewellery School, Florence, Italy · Founder, Opere International Jewellery School, Ravenstein, The Netherlands · **RP:** Gallery Rob Koudijs · Antonella Villanova · Gallery Caroline Van Hoek · Galerie Platina · Galerie Spektrum · Ornamentum Gallery · www.ruudtpeters.nl

SHARI PIERCE → 196

Munich, Germany

Own Workshop, Munich, Germany · **TG:** Guest Professor, Geneva University of Art and Design, Switzerland (2011) · Guest Professor, Rhode School of Art and Design, Providence, Rhode Island, USA · **RP:** Galerie Rob Koudijs · Jewelers' Werk Galerie · www.sharipierce.com

SUSAN PIETZSCH (in collaboration with Valentina Seidel) → 150

Berlin, Germany / Tokyo, Japan

Founder, Schmuck2 · **RP:** Oona Galerie · Gallery Sofie Lachaert · Gallery Deux Poissons · www.susanpietzsch.com

CAMILLA PRASCH → 159

Denmark, Copenhagen

RP: Galeria Norsu · Galerie Biró · Galerie Hilde Leiss · C.A.J. Gallery · Ornamentum Gallery · Julie's Artisans · camillaprasch@gmail.com

BEVERLEY PRICE → 124, 140

Johannesburg, South Africa

bevprice@telkomsa.net

KATJA PRINS → 162

Haarlem, The Netherlands

RP: Galerie Rob Koudijs · Klimt02 Gallery ·
Alternatives Gallery · Ornamentum Gallery ·
Chi ha paura…? · www.katjaprins.com

DOROTHEA PRÜHL → 128

Halle, Germany

RP: Galerie Marzee ·
www.dorothea-pruehl.de

RAMÓN PUIG CUYÀS → 163

Barcelona, Spain

TG: Head, Jewellery Department, Escola,
Massana, Barcelona, Spain · RP: Galerie
Marzee · Galerie Biró · Galerie Pilartz ·
Alternatives Gallery · Velvet da Vinci ·
Galerie Noel Guyomarc'h ·
www.puigcuyas2.blogspot.com ·
puigcuyas@gmail.com

WENDY RAMSHAW → 186, 223

London, United Kingdom

RP: Lesley Craze Gallery ·
www.ramshaw-watkins.com

MAH RANA → 143, 206, 231

London, United Kingdom

TG: Course Leader, MA Jewellery Design,
London Metropolitan University, London,
UK · RP: Klimt02 Gallery · Galerie SO ·
www.jewelleryislife.com

KAIRE RANNIK → 207

Tallinn, Estonia

RP: Group ffff, Estonia · Charon Kransen
Arts · www.hot.ee/groupffff ·
Kaire.Rannik@mail.ee

**RIBBONESIA [TORU
YOSHIKAWA]** → 202

Hokkaido, Japan

RP: Gallery Deux Poissons ·
www.ribbonesia.com

GILBERT RIEDELBAUCH → 176

Canberra, ACT, Australia

TG: Head of Core Studies and Design Arts,
ANU College of Arts and Social Sciences,
Canberra, ACT, Australia · RP: Workshop
Bilk · www.virtualterritory.wordpress.com

GERD ROTHMANN → 68, 146

Munich, Germany

RP: Galerie Biró · Ornamentum Gallery

PHILIP SAJET → 168

Latour de France, France

RP: Galerie Marzee · philipsajet@gmail.com

LUCY SARNEEL → 121, 160

Amsterdam, The Netherlands

TG: Jewellery Department, Gerrit Rietveld
Akademy, Amsterdam, The Netherlands ·
RP: Galerie Marzee · Charon Kransen
Arts · Gallery Funaki · l.sarneel@planet.nl

MARJORIE SCHICK → 125, 131

Pittsburg, Kansas, United States

TG: Professor of Art, Pittsburg State
University, Pittsburg, Kansas, USA ·
RP: Galerie Ra · mschick@pittstate.edu

BERNHARD SCHOBINGER
→ 133, 142, 185

Richterswil, Switzerland

RP: Galerie SO · www.schobinger.ch ·

CONSTANZE SCHREIBER
→ 74, 188

Munich, Germany

RP: Galerie Ra · Ornamentum Gallery ·
Klimt02 Gallery · Gallery Deux Poissons ·
www.constanzeschreiber.com

ROBERT SMIT → 182, 224

Amsterdam, The Netherlands

RP: Galerie Louise Smit

BETTINA SPECKNER → 84

Übersee, Germany

RP: Galerie Ra · Gallery Funaki ·
Galerie SO · Gallery Deux Poissons ·
www.bettina-speckner.com

HANS STOFER → 206

London, United Kingdom

TG: Professor and Head of Department,
Goldsmithing, Silversmithing, Metalwork
and Jewellery, Royal College of Art,
London, UK · RP: Galerie Marzee ·
Gallery SO · gsmj@rca.ac.uk ·
hans.stofer@rca.ac.uk

ANNELIES STRBA → 142

(in collaboration with Bernhard Schobinger)

Richterwil and Amden, Switzerland

www.strba.ch

BLANCHE TILDEN → 158

Melbourne, VIC, Australia

RP: Gallery Funaki · Workshop Bilk ·
www.blanchetilden.com.au

RACHEL TIMMINS → 71

Towson, Maryland, United States

TG: Graduate Assistant, Studio Tech,
Towson University, Towson, Maryland,
USA · www.racheltimmins.com

TJEK [FRANK TJEPKEMA] → 197

Amsterdam, The Netherlands

Partner (with Janneke Hooymans) ·
RP: Chi ha paura…? · www.tjep.com

**TOTA RECICLADOS
[VALERIA HASSE AND
MARCELA MUÑIZ]** → 129

Buenos Aires, Argentina

www.totareciclados.com.ar

MAUD TRAON → 52

London, United Kingdom

RP: Lesley Craze Gallery · Electrum Gallery ·
www.maudtraon.net

FABRIZIO TRIDENTI → 43

Vasto, Italy

www.fabriziotridenti.it

PETER TULLY (1947–1992) → 228,
229

Sydney, NSW, Australia / Paris, France

Artistic Director (1982–1986),
Sydney Gay & Lesbian Mardi Gras,
Sydney, NSW, Australia

MARK VAARWEK → 174

Sydney, NSW, Australia

RP: Workshop Bilk · www.vaarwek.com

WILLY VAN DE VELDE → 175

Schoten, Belgium

www.wvandevelde.be

FELIEKE VAN DER LEEST → 89

Øystese, Norway

RP: Galerie Rob Koudijs · Charon Kransen
Arts · Gallery Deux Poissons ·
www.feliekevanderleest.com

MANON VAN KOUSWIJK
→ 39, 191

Melbourne, VIC, Australia

RP: Gallery Funaki · Galerie Ra · Klimt02
Gallery · Gallery SO · Platina Gallery ·
Verzameld Werk · Gallery Deux Poissons ·
manon@hetnet.nl

LISA WALKER → 126

Wellington, New Zealand

RP: Galerie Biró · Fingers · Gallery Funaki ·
Jewelers'werk Galerie · Masterworks ·
Oona Galerie · Galeria Ra · Galerie
SO · Galerie Platina · Caroline Van Hoek
Gallery · www.lisawalker.de

DAVID WATKINS
→ 57, 110, 135, 146, 222

London, United Kingdom

www.ramshaw-watkins.com

MARGARET WEST → 92

Blackheath, NSW, Australia

margwest@optusnet.com.au

CHRISTOPH ZELLWEGER
→ 123

Zurich, Switzerland

TG: Professor of Art & Design, Sheffield
Hallam University, UK · Lecturer,
BA Design, Zurich University of the
Arts, Zurich, Switzerland · Lecturer,
MA Design, Lucerne School of Art
and Design, Lucerne, Switzerland ·
RP: Galerie Louise Smit ·
www.christophzellweger.com

Gallery Details

Alternatives Gallery, Rome, Italy
www.alternatives.it
Antonella Villanova, Florence, Italy
www.antonellavillanova.it
Atta Gallery, Bangkok, Thailand
www.attagallery.com
C.A.J. Gallery Kyoto, Japan
www.kondo-kyoto.com/caj
Caroline Van Hoek Gallery, Brussels, Belgium
carolinevanhoek.be
Charon Kransen Arts, New York, New York, USA
www.charonkransenarts.com
Chi ha paura…? Amsterdam, The Netherlands
www.chihapaura.com
Droog Design, New York, New York, USA
www.droog.com
Fingers Jewellery, Auckland, New Zealand
www.fingers.co.nz
Electrum Gallery, London, UK
www.electrumgallery.co.uk
Flow Gallery
www.flowgallery.co.uk
Four, Gothenburg, Sweden
www.foursweden.com
Galleria Norsu, Helsinki, Finland
www.norsu.info
Galerie Annick Zufferey, Carouge, Switzerland
www.galerie-annickzufferey.com
Galerie Aurum, Frankfurt, Germany
www.galerie-aurum.de
Galerie Beatrice Lang, Bern, Switzerland
www.beatricelan.ch
Galerie Biró, Munich, Germany
www.galerie-biro.de
Gallery Hélène Poree, France
www.galerie-helene-poree.com
Galerie Hilde Leiss, Hamburg, Germany
hilde-leiss.de
Galerie Louise Smit, Amsterdam, The Netherlands
www.louisesmit.nl
Galerie Marzee, Nijmegen, The Netherlands
www.marzee.nl
Galerie Noel Guyomarc'h, Montréal, Canada
www.galerienoelguyomarch.com
Galerie Pilartz, Cologne, Germany
www.pilartz.com
Galerie Platina, Stockholm, Sweden
www.platina.se
Galerie Ra, Amsterdam, The Netherlands
www.galerie-ra.nl

Galerie Reverso, Lisbon, Portugal
www.reversodasbernardas.com
Galerie Rob Koudijs, Amsterdam, The Netherlands
www.galerierobkoudijs.nl
Galerie Slavik, Vienna, Austria
www.galerie-slavik.com
Galerie SO, London, UK / Solothurn, Switzerland
www.galerieso.com
Galerie Sofie Lachaert, Tielrode, Belgium
www.lachaert.com
Galerie Spektrum, Munich, Germany
www.galerie-spektrum.de
Galerie Viceversa, Lausanne, Switzerland
www.viceversa.ch
Galerie V&V, Vienna, Austria
www.galerievundv.at
Galerie Wittenbrink, Munich, Germany
www.galeriewittenbrink.de
Gallery Deux Poissons, Tokyo, Japan
www.deuxpoissons.com
Gallery Funaki, Melbourne, VIC, Australia
www.galleryfunaki.com.au
Gallery Loupe, Montclair, New Jersey, USA
www.galleryloupe.com
Jewelers'werk Galerie, Washington, DC, USA
www.jewelerswerk.com
Julie: Artisans' Gallery, New York, New York, USA
www.julieartisans.com
Klimt02 Gallery, Barcelona, Spain
www.klimt02.net/gallery/
Lesley Craze Gallery, London, UK
www.lesleycrazegallery.co.uk
Marsden Woo Gallery, London, UK
www.marsdenwoo.com
Masterworks, Auckland, New Zealand
www.masterworksgallery.com
Maurer Zilioli Contemporary Arts, Brescia, Italy
www.maurerzilioli.com
Oona, Berlin, Germany
www.oona-galerie.de
Ornamentum Gallery, Hudson, Ohio, USA
www.ornamentumgallery.com
Pedras e Pêssegos, Porto, Portugal
www.pedrasepessegos.com
Sculpture to Wear, Santa Monica, California, USA
www.sculpturetowear.com
Sienna Gallery, Lenox, Massachusetts, USA
www.siennagallery.com
Snyderman Works Galleries, Philadelphia,
Pennsylvania, USA
www.snyderman-works.com
The Scottish Gallery, Edinburgh, UK
www.scottish-gallery.co.uk

Vallery, Barcelona, Spain
www.vallery.es
Velvet da Vinci, San Francisco, California, USA
www.velvetdavinci.com
Verzameld Werk, Ghent, Belgium
www.verzameldwerk.be
Workshop Bilk, Queanbeyan, NSW, Australia
www.workshopbilk.com

Image Credits

Image credits are listed alphabetically by photographer's surname with the exception of galleries/organisations, which are listed alphabetically by name.

Key: Numbers refer to page numbers

t=top, c=centre, b=bottom, l=left, r=right

© ADAGP, Paris and DACS, London 2011 (214)

© 2011 The Josef and Anni Albers Foundation/ Artists Rights Society, New York / Bild-Kunst, Germany (212)

Tobias Alm (194)

Miki Anagrius (165t)

Rebecca Annand (177t)

Gedusa Arndt (141, 172t)

Ton Baadenhuysem (62, 63)

Gijs Bakker (153r, 134)

Enrico Bartolucci (76, 82b, 197cl, 198t)

Rien Bazen (56t, 108, 176b, 178bl, 178br, 179t, 197t, 225)

Anna Beeke (109)

Courtesy of Friedman Benda (134)

Simon Bielander (44b, 203t)

Terence Bogue (67, 77b, 88t, 148l, 148r, 172b)

Nikolas Brade (168t)

Maisie Broadhead (138, 139)

Sigurd Bronger (184)

Mihai Burlacu (187)

Colin Campbell (206t)

Attai Chen (82t)

Norman Cherry (149l, 149r)

Simon Cottrell (162r)

Bob Cramp (186)

Dang-Vu Dang (53)

Paul Derrez (103t, 103b, 105, 106)

Jeremy Dillon (41t, 51b, 55t, 80, 86b, 169t, 178t, 180, 181, 198bl, 198br)

Georg Dobler (48)

Mason Douglas (196)

Paul Duvochel (83)

Dirk Eisel (45tl, 45tr)

Uta Eisenreich (39, 191t)

Angela Fisher (218, 219)

Bruce Fox (71)

Felix Flurry (133)

Karl Fritsch (55b, 190)

Kei Furuse (202t)

Susie Ganch (42)

Uri Geshuni (41c)

John Gollings (31tr, 31br)

Kate Gollings (145)

Christine Graf (164r)

Elisabeth Grebe (152t, 152b)

Tom Haartsen (81t, 130, 204)

Mike Hallson (147)

Jukka Halttunen (207t)

Sang-deok Han (201t)

Grant Hancock (40a, 200b)

Eddo Hartmann (74t, 89, 188t)

Ponch Hawkes (92t)

Robert Hensleigh (44t)

Herman Hermsen (79b)

Kurt Hess (90t)

Hogers/Versluys (104)

Myoungwook Huh (195tl, 195tr)

Julian Hutchens (41b, 200t)

Corinne Janier (85, 118l, 118c, 118r, 119)

Petra Jaschke (87)

Yong-il Jeon (170l)

Svenja John (56b)

Mathilde Jurrissen (153l)

Kimiaki Kageyama (86t)

Arne Kaiser (93)

© Lauren Kalman (97)

Jiro Kamata (43b, 69, 88b)

Beate Klockmann (168bl, 168br)

Eric Knoote (121, 160t)

Dorte Krogh (159t)

Johannes Kuhnen (166t, 171t)

Otto Künzli (75, 79t, 133, 144, 154, 155tl, 155tr, 155bl, 155br, 170r, 188b, 205t)

Gene Lee (202b)

Sari Liimatta (123)

Bas Linssen (45, 166b)

Fritz Maierhofer (49b)

Shannon McGarth (30)

Bruce Metcalf (189t)

Mikaela Mikhaylova (77t)

Taweesak Molsawat (54)

Marc Monzó (158t)

Shunichiro Nakashima (161t)

Iris Nieuwenburg (192b)

Courtesy Nogueras Blanchard, Barcelona (101)

Atelier Ted Noten (38tl, 38bl, 58, 59, 183)

Yagi Pardo (78)

Kwang-Chun Park (193b)

Wilfried Petzi (146)

Gary Pollmiller (99, 125, 131)

Bernd Preiml (127)

Beverley Price (124)

Ramón Puig Cuyàs (163t)

© Paco Rabanne/ Victoria and Albert Museum, London (217)

Mah Rana (143, 231)

Patrick Reynolds (51t, 90b)

Gilbert Riedelbauch (176t)

Maria Robledo (213)

Isamu Sawa (31tl)

Bernhard Schobinger (185)

Philipp Schönborn (68)

Marcus Scholz (158b)

Helga Schulze-Brinkop (128)

Valentina Seidel (150t, 150b, 151)

Mitsuo Shimada (164l)

James Shorrocks (52t)

Robert Smit (182, 224)

Deb Smith (66)

Garry Sommerfeld (National Gallery of Victoria) (222, 223, 226, 227, 228, 229)

Bettina Speckner (84t)

Kevin Sprague (192t)

Martijn Steiner Lovisa (102)

Hans Stofer (206b)

Harold Strak (120)

Annelies Strba (142l, 142r)

Des Tak (140)

© Yoshi Takata / Archive Pierre Cardin (216t)

Mirei Takeuchi (173t)

ten_do_ten (167)

Colin Thomas (14, 15t, 15b, 16, 17, 18, 20t, 20b, 21, 22, 23t, 23b, 24, 25, 28, 29)

Roy Tremain (45b)

Fabrizio Tridenti (43t)

Martin Tuma (81b)

Mark Vaarwek (174l, 174r)

Willy Van de Velde (175t)

Rob Versluys (49t)

Shadi Vossough (52b)

Lisa Walker (126)

David Ward (65, 91)

Damian Wasser (129)

David Watkins (57, 110, 135)

Margaret West (92b)

Guilerno White (47)

Francis Willemstijn (84b, 162l, 199t)

Christoph Zellweger (122t, 122b)

Ron Zijlstra (74b)

Reinhard Zimmermann (160b)

Notes

Chapter Two: Making, Wearing, Belonging

1   Andy Stafford and Michael Carter, (eds), *Roland Barthes: The Language of Fashion,* trans. Andy Stafford (Sydney: Power Publications, 2006), 63.

2   Ibid, 62.

3   Deyan Sudjic, *The Language of Things* (London: Penguin, 2009), 49.

4   Ibid, 49.

5   Ibid, 118.

6   Terry Smith, "Craft, Modernity and Postmodernity" in Sue Rowley (ed.), *Craft & Contemporary Theory* (St Leonards: Allen & Unwin, 1997), 20–21.

7   David Pye, "The Nature and Art of Workmanship" in Glenn Adamson (ed.), *The Craft Reader* (Oxford: Berg 2010), 345.

8   Ibid, 341.

9   Christopher Lasch, *The Minimal Self: Psychic Survival in Troubled Times* (New York: W.W. Norton, 1984), 32–34.

10 Christine Boyer, *Cybercities: Visual Perception in the Age of Electronic Communication* (New York: Princeton Architectural Press, 1996), 10.

11 Maurice Merleau-Ponty, *The Phenomenology of Perception*, 165.

12 Ibid.

13 Ida van Zijl, *Gijs Bakker and Jewellery* (Stuttgart: Arnoldsche Art Publishers, 2005), 146.

14 Helen Drutt English and Peter Dormer, *Jewellery of Our Time: Art, Ornament and Obsession* (London: Thames and Hudson, 1995), 107.

15 Dorothea Mink, "Fashion: The Language of the Self" in Eike Bippus and Dorothea Mink (eds.), *Fashion Body Cult* (Stuttgart: Arnoldsche Art Publishers, 2007), 276.

16 Ibid, 274.

17 Roland Barthes, *The Fashion System* trans. Matthew Wards and Richard Howard (Los Angeles: University of California Press 1990), 258–259.

18 Georg Simmel, "Adornment" in David Frisby and Mike Featherstone (eds.), *Simmel on Culture* (London: Sage Publications, 1997), 206.

19 Phyllis Grosskurth, *The Secret Ring: Freud's Inner Circle and the Politics of Psychoanalysis* (Reading: Addison-Wesley, 1991), 57.

Chapter Three: Metal Against the Body

1   Rose Slivka, "Review: Britain Salutes New York Festival", *Crafts* 64 (September/October 1983), pp. 44–5: 45.

2   Peter Dormer, "Dyed in the Wool", *Crafts* 69 (July/August 1984), pp.12–13: 12.

3   Ben Lignel, e-mail to the author, 24 July 2011.

4   Gabriel Craig, "The Transgressions of Lauren Kalman," *American Craft* (Oct/Nov. 2009), p. 40.

5   Ben Lignel, e-mail to the author, 28 July 2011.

Chapter Eight: A Brief Contemporary Jewellery History

1   Barbara Cartlidge, *Twentieth-Century Jewellery.* (New York: Harry N. Abrams, 1985); Alexander Rower and Holton Rower (ed.), *Calder Jewellery* (New York: Calder Foundation, 2007).

2   Helen Drutt and Peter Dormer, *Jewellery of Our Time,* 24.

3   Ibid, 19.

4   For details on the influence and importance of Hermann Jünger, refer to the list of major jewellery books outlined at the beginning of these endnotes. For references which solely detail Jünger's work, refer to Florian Hufnagl (ed.), *Found Treasures Hermann: Jünger and the Art of Jewellery* (London: Thames & Hudson, 2003); Florian Hufnagl (ed.), *Hermann Jünger: Jewellery—Found Objects* (Mainz: Verlag Hermann Schmidt, 2002).

5   Peter Dormer and Ralph Turner, *The New Jewellery*, 15.

6   Ibid, 22–24.

7   Ralph Turner, "The Golden Years?" in Paul Derrez (ed.), *Radiant: 30 years Ra* (Amsterdam: Galerie Ra, 2006), 11.

8   Peter Dormer and Ralph Turner, *The New Jewellery*, 182.

9   Brian Turner, *Regulating Bodies: Essays in Medical Sociology* (London: Routledge, 1992), 164–166.

10 Peter Dormer and Ralph Turner, *The New Jewellery*, 49–150.

11 Helen Drutt and Peter Dormer, *Jewellery of Our Time*, 27.

12 Peter Dormer and Ralph Turner, *The New Jewellery*, 182.

13 Ibid, 7.

14 For reflections on how Walter Benjamin's studies on the value of art in the age of technical reproducibility extended into the cultural logic of postmodernism, see Andrew Benjamin (ed.), *Walter Benjamin and Art* (London: Continuum, 2005).

Acknowledgements

Susan Cohn would like to thank the following people for their invaluable support on this project over an extended period of time.

To Deyan Sudjic, director of the Design Museum, for asking me to curate this exhibition as well as edit this book, and for his ongoing intellectual stimulation; Nina Due, head of exhibitions at the Design Museum, for her patience, support and expertise with managing this complex project; Guilia Ascoli, Design Museum research assistant, for persistently sourcing material. To Francis Lindsay, deputy director of the National Gallery of Victoria, for enabling this exhibition to happen in Melbourne; Nicole Monteiro, head of exhibitions, for her support and coordination.

Of course, this exhibition and book would never have happened without the creativity and dedication of contemporary jewellers. To all the selected jewellers, for lending their work and photographs, and also for their ongoing goodwill in dealing with my constant harassment for yet more, always urgent, information. To all those jewellers who sent detailed submissions but missed out due to the limitations of the exhibition, for their invaluable support in busy times.

To the other writers in the book, Glenn Adamson and Liesbeth den Besten, who contributed at short notice in the midst of curating their own major exhibitions, for adding other perceptive voices to the discussion. To other collaborators, Ab Rogers, for his inventive installation design, and Jonathan Abbott for his patient support in the graphic design of this book. To all the individuals and contemporary jewellery galleries who have contributed in various ways for their insight during the research process and for their support in the organisation procedures, especially Paul Derrez, Mah Rana, Helen Drutt English, Otto Künzli, Gijs Bakker, Felix Flury and Damian Skinner.

For his enthusiasm, dedication and camaraderie, my deepest thanks to the ghost, Michael Falk, whose writing and editing skills have helped me turn abstract words into writing, for his intellectual rapport, which has provided invaluable stimulus for consolidating ideas.

For their friendship and support over the call of duty, my thanks to Sarah Miller and Fiona McLean, for providing a room to stay with all the benefits of a household. Finally, for enduring this everlasting project, my heartfelt thanks to John Denton, the hub in my life, for tolerating the full spectrum of project emotions yet still readily supporting my every need.

Exhibition Lenders

In addition to the individual jewellers who have generously lent their work to this exhibition, we wish to thank the following lenders:

Public Institutions

National Gallery of Victoria
Melbourne, Australia
(Junger, p. 227; Künzli, p. 226;
Ramshaw, p. 223; Tully, p. 227, p.
228; Watkins, p. 222)
www.ngv.vic.gov.au

Powerhouse Museum
Sydney, Australia
www.powerhousemuseum.com

Stedelijk Museum
's–Hertogenbosch, The Netherlands
www.sm-s.nl

British Crafts Council
London, UK
www.craftscouncil.org.uk

Private Collectors

Elizabeth Argo
Susan Cummins
Paul Derrez and Willem Hoogstade
Helen Drutt English
Marian Fulk
Susan Kempin
Andrea Mignicci
Helena and Lasse Palhman
Anna Schwartz

Private Galleries

Caroline Van Hoek Gallery
Brussels, Belgium
carolinevanhoek.be

Friedman Benda
(Sottsass, p. 215)
New York, New York, USA
www.friedmanbenda.com

Galerie Louise Smit
Amsterdam, The Netherlands
www.louisesmit.nl

Galerie Marzee
Nijmegen, The Netherlands
www.marzee.nl

Galerie Ra
Amsterdam, The Netherlands
www.galerie-ra.nl

Galerie SO
London, UK / Solothurn, Switzerland
www.galerieso.com

Gallery Loupe
Montclair, New Jersey, USA
www.galleryloupe.com

Sienna Gallery, Lenox,
Massachusetts, USA
www.siennagallery.com

Velvet da Vinci, San Francisco,
California, USA
www.velvetdavinci.com

Susan Cohn is a contemporary jeweller, designer and curator.
She is director of Workshop 3000, has a Doctor of Philosophy
in Fine Art Theory and is represented by Anna Schwartz Gallery,
Melbourne, Australia.

Deyan Sudjic is director of the Design Museum in London.
His career has spanned journalism, teaching and writing.
He was director of Glasgow UK City of Architecture 1999 and
in 2002 he was Director of the Venice Architecture Biennale.

First published in the United States of America in 2012 by
RIZZOLI INTERNATIONAL PUBLICATIONS, INC.
300 Park Avenue South
New York, NY 10010
www.rizzoliusa.com

ISBN-13: 978-0-8478-3814-1
Library of Congress Control Number: 2011943317

Editor: Dung Ngo
Design: Jonathan Abbott at Barnbrook
Exhibition management: Nina Due
Research: Giulia Ascoli

Distributed to the U.S. trade by Random House, New York

Printed and bound in China

2012 2013 2014 2015 / 10 9 8 7 6 5 4 3 2 1